I AM

I AM

Summer McKinney

WordCrafts

I AM
Copyright © 2017
Summer McKinney

Cover design by David Warren

All rights reserved. No part of this book may be reproduced, stored in a retrieval system, or transmitted in any form or by any means – electronic, mechanical, photocopy, recording, or otherwise – without the prior written permission of the publisher. The only exception is brief quotations for review purposes.

Unless otherwise noted all Scripture quotations are taken from THE HOLY BIBLE, NEW INTERNATIONAL VERSION®, NIV® Copyright © 1973, 1978, 1984, 2011 by Biblica, Inc.™ Used by permission. All rights reserved worldwide.

Scripture quotations marked ESV are from the ESV® Bible (The Holy Bible, English Standard Version®), copyright © 2001 by Crossway, a publishing ministry of Good News Publishers. Used by permission. All rights reserved.

Scripture quotations marked CSB are from the Christian Standard Bible. Copyright © 2017 by Holman Bible Publishers. Used by permission. Christian Standard Bible®, and CSB® are federally registered trademarks of Holman Bible Publishers, all rights reserved.

Published by WordCrafts Press
Buffalo, WY 82834
www.wordcrafts.net

To Zakyra McKinney, Kari Harrison, and my former high school girls at CFC who have since grown into beautiful women of God.

CONTENTS

I AM 1

Created for relationships 15

Unique in Design 22

Living in our design 27

In need of a Savior 47

Redeemed and restored in righteousness 59

Our value, worth, and purpose 75

Living out your faith 91

Everything is for God's glory 119

Continue living in the Word 128

Acknowledgment 132

About the Author 133

I AM

Before we can begin with who we are, we must know who God is. This is the foundation for why we were created. Like all things God created, we are to bring Him glory. He delights in us and takes pleasure in us as His creation.

Many people struggle with that truth and question why God would choose them, value them, or want to have a relationship with them. The truth is that God loves us and no matter what we do. Those who have put their faith in Christ will never fall out of His grace. We cannot do anything to make God love us more, or ever do anything to make God love us less. We are His, and He not only created us, but when we (mankind) sinned against God, He purchased us back into a relationship with Him through His own blood sacrifice.

So, who is God?

If we look at Exodus 3:1-11, we will see an exchange between God and Moses that leads to this very question. Moses had fled from Egypt and was living in the wilderness when he encountered God. God told Moses to go to back to Egypt, tell Pharaoh to free the Israelites, and lead them into the promised land.

The next words out of Moses' mouth were, "Who am I that I should go to Pharaoh and bring the Israelites out of Egypt?" Moses did not see the same value in himself as God saw in him. He lacked the confidence and belief that his life had a greater purpose. God then responds with reassurance telling Moses that He will be with him.

Many of us, like Moses, doubt ourselves and sometimes fall prey to the lie that we can't do the task at hand, don't measure up, or are incompetent. God's response to Moses was perfect; it was the truth that he (man) must put faith in God and have confidence that He has already gone ahead of him, of all of us, and prepared the way. It is the truth that God has great plans and a purpose for us if we will be obedient to follow and trust that He will give us the strength, confidence, and power to complete the task.

This is not because God can't do it Himself, but rather God gets glory when we know it is because of Him that we are able to do great things.

Who *is* God? Well, if we keep reading in Exodus 3:12-15, Moses asks that same question.

> *And God said, "I will be with you. And this will be the sign to you that it is I who have sent you: When you have brought the people out of Egypt, you will worship God on this mountain."*
>
> *Moses said to God, "Suppose I go to the Israelites and say to them, 'The God of your fathers has sent me to you,' and they ask me, 'What is his name?' Then what shall I tell them?"*
>
> *God said to Moses, "I AM WHO I AM. This is what you are to say to the Israelites: 'I AM has sent me to you.'"*
>
> *God also said to Moses, "Say to the Israelites, 'The LORD, the God of your fathers—the God of Abraham, the God of Isaac and the God of Jacob—has sent me to you.'*
>
> *"This is my name forever, the name you shall call me from generation to generation."*

God's response is a loaded answer. "*I am who I am.*" Such a short sentence, but what power, authority, confidence, and depth is packed into it. "*I am*" is a personal identification, no different than if someone asks you who you are. You may say; *I am a girl, I am a man, I am a human being, I am an American*, or any other form of self-identification. God is bringing awareness to Moses. He is revealing who He is.

Another thing God said was, "Tell them the Lord, the God of your fathers …" This is important because God is stating his authority as Lord and as God. There are many "gods" that have been created by people and cultures over the span of time, but there is only one God of this universe, because it is God who created and rules over the universe, including all that inhabits it. He is called Lord because He has all power, authority, and influence.

Man did not name God. God is who He is because of who He is. God didn't inherit the title from someone else or create it Himself; it is exactly *who* He is. We can call a cat a dog, but it doesn't make it a dog. God is God, not because He chose to be, worked to be, or changed Himself to be. He is God because that *is* who He is. Once we recognize and acknowledge that, then we can start the journey of who we are.

God is holy, completely void of sin, and perfect. He is more than the things He does or the title we give; just as a person is more than a parent, spouse, sibling, teacher, lawyer, doctor, or friend. He is a triune God, which means He is three persons within one being, not three separate gods. We say "persons" because He has attributes of personhood which are displayed through each Father, Son, and Spirit.

There are passages of scripture where one person is called "God" or "the Lord" and it is distinguished from another person who is also said to be God. We can read about this in Psalm 45:6-7, where the Psalmist says,

> *"Your throne, O God, will last forever and ever ... You love righteousness and hate wickedness; therefore God, your God, has set you above your companions by anointing you with the oil of joy."*

The psalmist recognizes that there is one God, and in this verse, we can see he is also recognizing two separate persons as God.

We find in the New Testament that this passage is referring to Jesus Christ as Hebrews 8:1 says,

> *"Now the main point of what we are saying is this: We do have such a high priest, who sat down at the right hand of the throne of the Majesty in heaven,"*

We also see that there is one God with separate persons by looking at Psalm 110:1 where David says,

> *"The Lord says to my Lord: 'Sit at my right hand until I make your enemies a footstool for your feet.'"*

God the Father is telling God the Son to sit at His right hand. No one but God is equal to God.

We see the third person of God from the very beginning when the Old Testament refers to the "angel of the Lord" or a "messenger" of the Lord. This angel is a distinct being; however, at various points the angel is also referred to as God or the Lord. Isaiah 63:10 also mentions this third person of God when God's people rebelled and God said it "grieved his Holy Spirit." The fact that the Holy Spirit grieved suggests an emotional characteristic of a distinct person.

In the New Testament, we see even more confirmations of God's divine Trinity. When Jesus was baptized, Matthew 3:16-27 says,

> *"As soon as Jesus was baptized, He went up out of the water. At that moment heaven was opened, and He saw the Spirit of God descending like a dove and alighting on Him. And a voice from heaven said, 'This is my Son, whom I love; with Him I am well pleased.'"*

Within this passage we not only see the recognition of three distinct beings, we also see how each take part in activities and have roles or functions. God the Son is being baptized and God the Holy Spirit enlightens him, while God the Father speaks his pleasure, approval, and love towards him.

1 Corinthians 12:4-6 says,

> *"There are different kinds of gifts, but the same Spirit distributes them. There are different kinds of service, but the same Lord. There are different kinds of working, but in all of them and in everyone it is the same God at work."*

Ephesians 4:4-6 says,

> *"There is one body and one Spirit, just as you were called to one hope when you were called; one Lord, one faith, one baptism; one God and Father of all, who is over all and through all and in all."*

In the New Testament "God" typically refers to the Father and "Lord" refers to the Son. Over and over again we see in scripture the plurality of persons that make our one God.

More than a word can describe

There is no simple word or description to define God. Even our

English vocabulary is limited in its terminology. For example, did you know that in our English vocabulary there is only one word for love, but in Hebrew and Greek there are different words to describe different types of love? We love sunny days just as we love our best friend or chocolate. We may feel an emotional connection to one over another, but the terminology is still the same and does not reflect the varying depth of that love.

The Old Testament uses Hebrew words such as, "ahab," which is like a covenantal love, expressing desire and strong emotional attachment. Another word is "Ahabah" which describes God's love for His people even when they do not obey Him and choose to do wrong. "Habab" expresses God's cherishing of His people. It is a tender and protective love. "Hashaq" is God's attachment of love towards us. He longs for us, yearning for us to be connected and in a relationship with Him. "Hesed" describes God's character of love in that He is faithful, merciful, patient, gives loving kindness, and offers redemption. Even though someone doesn't deserve that kindness, it is given anyways.

The Hebrew language of the Old Testament is not the only one that has multiple words and meanings for a term. The Greek language, which is found in the New Testament, also has different words for different degrees of devotion and love.

There are six Greek words for love. In the New Testament, we see the Greek word "Agape" which is like a parental type of love. It is a selfless love from which we get our word "charity." Agape is not just for family, but a regard for all people.

"Eros" is another Greek word for love which is the type of love between two lovers. It is a passionate and physical type of love. It is also a dangerous love where one is irrational and loses control.

"Philia" is a friendship love. It is where Philadelphia, or 'city of brotherly love,' gets its name. It is one of comradeship, where brother in arms would fight and die side by side. It is about loyalty and sacrifice. "Ludus" means to be playful. It is to laugh, dance, joke, play, flirt, and have friendly bantering.

"Pragma" is the type of love that is developed between seasoned married couples. It is long withstanding and is about making an effort to give love rather than just receiving it. The final type of love the Greeks identified is "Philautia" which is a love of the self. This can be a negative narcissistic type of love in which one is obsessed with his/her own personhood, or it can be a healthy love in which one is so secure and confident with him/herself that he has plenty of love to give.

All these words and meanings make up our one word: "love." It's no wonder so much meaning is lost when we are limited on words to describe something that is much more. So, how does this fit into who God is?

We need to realize that the very phrase God used to call Himself, "I am," has much more meaning than what one may perceive. Just as the word "love" has such depth and richness beyond the term itself, there are also character traits of God that are evident and go deeper in understanding. As we read scripture we learn more about God's character, which reveals more about who God is. As we pursue a relationship with God, we experience more of who God is and see more of his character.

Another reason for bringing up the varying definitions of love is because God is love. 1 John 4:7-8 says,

> *"Dear friends, let us love one another, for love comes from God. Everyone who loves has been born of God and knows God. Whoever does not love does not know God, because God is love."*

If it were not for God's love, we would be condemned to eternity in hell.

> "But because of his great love for us, God, who is rich in mercy, made us alive with Christ even when we were dead in transgressions—it is by grace you have been saved."
>
> Ephesians 2:4-5

We are to represent the love of God in each of our relationships. It may be the playful or brotherly love amongst friends, the passionate and committed love to a spouse, the secure and confident love in ourselves, or the forgiving and gracious love to someone who has wounded us.

My favorite passage in scripture is in Proverbs 27:19. It says,

> *"As water reflects a face, so a man's heart reflects the man."*

I like this verse because of its truth that character, integrity, and intentions flow out of the heart and are evident in how we act, behave, or respond to people in the world around us. The more we read, hear about, and experience God's character, the more we know about who He is and the more we can trust and rely on Him because He is faithful, righteous, pure and He knows us better than we know ourselves. Galatians 5:22-23 says,

> *"The fruit of the spirit is joy, love, peace, forbearance, kindness, goodness, faithfulness, gentleness, and self-control."*

God not only *is* each of these, He has also *given* each of us possession of these characteristics and we have a responsibility to extend them to others as we interact with each other.

Made in His image

The book of Genesis is where we must first look to find out how and why we were created. This is important because all creation has a purpose, and that purpose helps define who we are. Genesis is where we find the beginning of our existence and where we are appointed certain tasks and responsibilities.

This is also the origin of our relational dynamics that affect positively and negatively our interactions with each other, especially regarding the opposite sex.

> *"Then God said, 'Let us make mankind in our image, in our likeness, so that they may rule over the fish in the sea and the birds in the sky, over the livestock and all the wild animals, and over all the creatures that move along the ground.'"*
>
> Genesis 1:26

The first thing to notice here are the words "us" and "our." God as the Father, the Son, and the Holy Spirit made mankind, together, each being actively involved and each creating man with His own attributes.

The second thing to notice is that we were made. If we look earlier in the chapter where God created light, water, sky, and land, they were all spoken into existence. With mankind, God didn't just speak him into existence, God took an active role and "made" him.

This action verb indicates that God put thought, effort, creativity, and time into forming, molding, and designing man just the way He wanted. God just didn't create man at random or with odd features, God was intentional in how He created. God took dust on the ground, something we view as dirty, not good, or something to discard, and made something wonderful.

This can be a reminder that no matter what things we have done, or how mucky our lives have become, God can turn our lives into something good.

God also took a rib from the man and made woman. We will discuss this more later, but it is important to again note how God intentionally created mankind out of something that we can easily overlook as having meaning and value.

The third thing to notice in this passage is that man was created for a purpose. God gave mankind roles and responsibilities, and we are held accountable for these tasks.

> *Then the Lord God formed a man from the dust of the ground and breathed into his nostrils the breath of life, and the man became a living being.*
> Genesis 2:7

God not only formed man, God also gave life to man. He didn't *speak* life into man; God again took action and *breathed* His own life into man, giving man his first heartbeat.

When someone is not breathing, we give what is called rescue breaths. Our mouth covers the person's mouth and our breath fills his/her lungs providing the oxygen needed to sustain vital organs. How cool is it to know that God gave man his very first breath from His own breath? God is our life supply and through Him we not only have life, but because of Jesus we have eternal life.

> *"So God created mankind in his own image, in the image of God he created them; male and female he created them."*
> Genesis 1:27

It is important to look at how we were made—in the image of God, in his likeness. God created the animals and mankind; however, unlike the animals, God made us in his image. When sin came into the picture, mankind's image was distorted as man's moral purity was compromised. Through Jesus we see our human likeness to God as it was intended to be. We can find joy in the fact that we are predestined to be conformed to the image of Jesus and even though the full measure of our image, as was originally designed, has been distorted by the sin of man; we are still like God, represent God, and will one day be restored to our original and full design.

We, like our Creator, have spiritual aspects. We have a physical body that, due to sin, will fade away. However, we also have a spirit which, like God, is eternal. God created us with a spirit so that we can relate to Him and spend eternity with Him.

God also created angels and other heavenly creatures as spiritual beings; however, we are the only creation He made that has a physical and spiritual body.

In addition to being spiritually in God's image, we are also intellectually made in His image. Angels and humans are the only moral and highly-intelligent creatures God created. Unlike animals, we have the ability to reason, think, and learn. It is true that there are intelligent animals, intelligence being ranked within the animal kingdom category; however, when compared to a human, they are vastly limited. An animal may solve a puzzle, run a maze, or learn to sign to communicate, but you will never have a deep philosophical conversation with an animal or discuss the meaning of life, dreams, or technological advances. We are truly created different and with a higher purpose.

We each possess attributes of God. These attributes and character or personality traits of God are evident throughout scripture. Compassion, care, humility, love, and kindness, as well as strength, discipline, will, and wisdom are a few of those character traits. There are communicable and incommunicable attributes of God. This means that there are attributes that are specific to God alone (incommunicable) such as His omniscience, power, transcendence, or self-existence. And there are those attributes he shares with us (communicable) such as His goodness, wisdom, or holiness.

This is not an exhaustive list, and we should note that there is not an absolute line between the two categories. Holiness is to be without sin or blame and unlike us, God is inherently holy. However, because of Jesus and the Spirit of God dwelling in us, we are to strive for holiness and set ourselves apart. In Leviticus 19:2, God tells his people to,

> *"Be holy because I, the Lord your God, am holy."*

In our life stages, we can relate to these different attributes of God and how our identity is found in the root of God as our Creator. Some of these attributes align perfectly within roles, responsibilities, or giftings that we are given. When you get married, you gain a deeper understanding of your relationship with Jesus as our bridegroom. When you become a parent, you gain a deeper insight into your relationship with God as the Father. When you go through hurts and pains of this broken world, you gain a deeper awareness of the Spirit in how He comforts and guides.

To glorify Him

Now that we know the image in whom God created us, the question of "why?" still remains. God did not need to create man; however, He chose to create man and in doing so, it brought Him glory. Ephesians 1:11-12 says,

> *"In Him we were also chosen, having been predestined according to the plan of Him who works out everything in conformity with the purpose of his will, in order that*

we, who were the first to put our hope in Christ, might be for the praise of His glory."

As we will read later, God uses the uniqueness in which He has made us, the attributes He has given us, along with our personality, giftings, and talents to bring Him glory.

As we find joy, significance, and dignity in our making in the likeness of God, we also need to remember that we are flawed and marred by sin. Before God even created us, He knew we would need a savior.

We were created perfect—however, sin distorted our perfection and put a divide in our relationship with God. It is important to recognize our need for a savior and understand our own depravity, which we will discuss more on later; but, we must also come to know our worth and value. We are created even more special than the stars in the sky, more remarkable than the expanse of the universe, and even more valuable than all other living creatures in this world. Even the most sinful man, the vilest person we can think of is also created in the image of God.

Wayne Grudem says it this way:

> *"Every single human being, no matter how much the image of God is marred by sin, or illness, or weakness, or age, or any other disability, still has the status of being in God's image and therefore must be treated with dignity and respect that is due to God's image bearer."*

This means the mentally ill, the elderly, the disabled, the annoying know-it-alls, nagging wives, inattentive husbands, nosey neighbors, etc., all deserve to be treated with the honor and respect of being human. Character respect is earned, but respect for human life is automatically granted, whether it's an unborn life, a "wasted" life on drugs and cheap thrills, or any other lifestyle one chooses.

Being an image-bearer of God means we know who created us, and we represent Him by living out His character attributes and offer love, mercy, and grace to others. It is when we reject our status that we depreciate our own value and worth, as well as human life in general. When that happens, one will start to believe and view human life as being nothing more than an evolved animal, with no purpose or meaning, just existing, and will begin to treat others with that same attitude.

We are more than animals. We are called to a higher purpose. Unlike all other creation, we are created in God's image and we possess His attributes. As God is relational, we too, are created for relationships. To have great relationships with others, we must value life and understand that we are created in His image, and not just by possessing some of His attributes. We are created in his image spiritually, morally, mentally, and relationally, and through these we can display those deeper character attributes of God that we also possess.

CREATED FOR RELATIONSHIPS

Before we can dive further into *how* God created man and woman in relation to our role and purpose, we must look at *why* God created man and then created woman, as well as the relationship between them. As we already know, God created all things, including man, for His glory.

When He was done creating, He said, "It is good." God was glorified and all creation brought Him glory just by existing.

Humans can continue to choose to bring God glory through our relationship with Him. This is the other reason why we are created; to be in relationship with God. If you think about the nature of God, He is inherently relational due to the very existence of the Trinity. The Father, Son, and Spirit are always interacting with each other. Likewise, God created us to be in relationship with Him. He pursues us and desires a relationship with us as His creation.

Can you imagine what it must have been like to be Adam? Here you are, standing in front of the One who created you, and it is a perfect relationship. I believe they took walks together, and that God showed Adam all the wondrous things He created.

Picture how it must have been for God to lead Adam to different places, things, creatures small and large, gigantic trees, lush greenery, majestic stars, skies that expanded beyond the eye can see, colors in various hues of the rainbow, fruit so plump and juicy, water so clear and fresh. Adam's eyes must have lit up in amazement and his mouth smiled in excitement and awe at the amazing creations.

The fascination of all that was in front of Adam was, I bet, more than the bewilderment of a little girl at Disney's Princess Palace, or the amazement of a little boy watching the biggest fireworks show for the first time. Here is the Creator Himself, sharing creation with Adam, and giving him free reign to explore it all.

What kind of talks did they have? Did they talk about God's creations, or perhaps laugh at some of the funny designs, smells, or looks of some of the animals? Did Adam race Jesus through the garden and give the Father hugs? Did they explore together? Did God smile at Adam's curiosity and fascination with creation? We don't know all that took place, but we do know that their relationship was perfect and that Adam gave glory to God and God was pleased by him.

God is relational. God created mankind to be in relationship with Him first, and then with each other. The relationship God had with Adam, and then Eve, was perfect—until sin entered the heart of man.

There are many times in our lives when we feel distant from God, or our relationship with God is neglected. It is important to remember that God isn't the one who leaves or abandons us; we are the ones who put a wedge in the relationship. Sometimes the wedge is from our own guilt or shame. Sometimes we have a conviction of sin and don't want to go to God to face the conviction or admit the wrong. Sometimes we know how we should act toward someone. Sometimes we know exactly what God wants us to do in a situation and we flat out don't want to obey—like Jonah, who knew God wanted him to tell the Ninevites about Him, yet Jonah did not want them to be saved, so he ran from God.

This wedge in our relationship can also stem from faulty perceptions of God, such as God being one who is waiting to pounce on every wrong. This wedge can stem from having poor models of parents growing up, having fathers who neglect or reject, or having a church leader who spiritually abused scripture of who God is in order to have "good" followers. It is easy for us to project those same feelings or thoughts towards God. After all, He reveals Himself as our "Heavenly Father."

This wedge can stem from shame. Perhaps we feel unworthy, undeserving, or have not forgiven ourselves and can't accept that God has forgiven us, wants us, loves us or values us.

God desires to have relationship with us, and just as we pursue relationships with our friends, children, and spouse, He also pursues us. Similar to how we grow our relationships with others, we must reciprocate and pursue back. Relationships aren't one-sided. However, unlike man's natural tendency towards sin and isolation, God will never stop pursuing us.

It saddens Him when we reject Him, ignore Him, or don't engage in relationship with Him, but no matter how we have responded to Him, He is always with us and is delighted when we do turn to Him and pursue relationship back with Him. As with any relationship, we need to actively engage in it and grow it, otherwise it will become stale or fade.

Relationships with others

God not only created us to be in relationship with Him, but like the relationship of the Trinity, He wants us to be in relationship with each other.

> *"This is the account of the heavens and the earth when they were created, when the Lord God made the earth*

and the heavens. Now no shrub had yet appeared on the earth and no plant had yet sprung up, for the Lord God had not sent rain on the earth and there was no one to work the ground, but streams came up from the earth and watered the whole surface of the ground. Then the Lord God formed a man from the dust of the ground and breathed into his nostrils the breath of life, and the man became a living being.

Now the Lord God had planted a garden in the east, in Eden; and there He put the man He had formed. The Lord God made all kinds of trees grow out of the ground—trees that were pleasing to the eye and good for food. In the middle of the garden were the tree of life and the tree of the knowledge of good and evil."

Genesis 2:4-9

"The Lord God took the man and put him in the Garden of Eden to work it and take care of it. And the Lord God commanded the man, 'You are free to eat from any tree in the garden; but you must not eat from the tree of the knowledge of good and evil, for when you eat from it you will certainly die.'

The Lord God said, "It is not good for the man to be alone. I will make a helper suitable for him."

Now the Lord God had formed out of the ground all the wild animals and all the birds in the sky. He brought them to the man to see what he would name them; and whatever the man called each living creature, that was its name. So the man gave names to all the livestock, the birds in the sky and all the wild animals.

But for Adam no suitable helper was found. So the Lord God caused the man to fall into a deep sleep; and while he was sleeping, He took one of the man's ribs and then closed up the place with flesh. Then the Lord God

> *made a woman from the rib he had taken out of the man, and He brought her to the man.*
>
> Genesis 2:15-22

When God first created Adam, He was pleased with him and gave him the responsibility to rule over the land, work and care for the ground, and tend to the animals. God brought the animals to Adam and gave him the honor of naming them.

God created each animal male and female, but I believe He intentionally created Adam without a female counterpart at first. God knew it was not good for man to be alone, but man needed to come to this realization himself. It was important for Adam to see and feel the loss of companionship compared with what all the other creatures had. God wanted and allowed this to happen because when we personally experience something, it takes on a deeper awareness and appreciation than when someone just tells us we need something or are missing something of value. Once Adam had an awareness, yearning and desire for a companion, God created Eve.

Why did God say it wasn't good for man to be alone if God was there with Adam and they had a perfect relationship? Adam needed a companion who was *like* him. Man is God's creation, and though God deeply loves and cares for us and gave us His attributes, we will never be *fully* like God. God knew that it was best for man to have a companion who was like him (man), so they could share in God's creations together.

So, God presented Eve to Adam and in keeping with the responsibility Adam was given, he named his female counterpart—*Woman*.

> "The man said, 'This is now bone of my bones and flesh of my flesh; she shall be called 'woman,' for she was taken out of man.'"

> *That is why a man leaves his father and mother and is united to his wife, and they become one flesh."*
>
> Genesis 2:23-24

> *"God blessed them and said to them, 'Be fruitful and increase in number; fill the earth and subdue it. Rule over the fish in the sea and the birds in the sky and over every living creature that moves on the ground.'"*
>
> Genesis 1:28

It is part of God's nature to create, and it was His intention that His creations bring Him glory. Creating man and woman, and equipping them with feelings of desire, passion, love, and the ability to reproduce and create through His intricate design another human being, brings Him glory.

It also brings him glory when men and women work together within the design in which God created them. Like Adam's relationship with God, Eve's relationship with God was perfect, and their relationship together was perfect. There was no shame as they stood naked before each other; there was no fear of vulnerability with each other, just complete trust. There was no view of one being weaker than the other or denigration due to their differences. All of those relational wedges came after sin entered the picture.

We get glimpses of what it must have been like during those moments when our marital relationship is sacrificially loving and selflessly giving in accordance to God's original design; when we are working together with others and encouraging them rather than feeling threatened by their strengths or abilities that we may not possess.

Before sin, there was perfection in all aspects of man and woman's relationship: their design, their roles, and how these things worked together in bringing God glory. There was perfection in their relationship with

God and how together they worked within their design to please Him. That perfection was to be carried out in their children and the children from generations to come.

Even though sin changed the perfect relationship we had with God and each other, it is important to remember that God did not model abandonment. God didn't say, "Well, I guess I better scrap Adam and Eve and start again." No, God continued to be in relationship with us and through Jesus gave us hope of an eternally and perfectly restored relationship with Him.

He even modeled through Jesus how to be in and even repair our relationship with each other as we interact together in a broken world. In Matthew 22:37-39, Jesus says we must,

> *"Love the Lord [our] God with all [our] heart and with all [our] soul and with all [our] mind. This is the first and greatest commandment. And the second is like it: 'Love your neighbor as yourself.'"*

We must love God first, respond to His pursuit of a relationship with each of us and grow in what it means to be His. Then we can learn and understand more about what it means to live in accordance with His design and how that plays out in our relationship with each other.

UNIQUE IN DESIGN

As you read the next couple of sections discussing our design and roles as male and female, it is important to keep a biblical mind and a biblical worldview, rather than a fleshly mind and worldly perspective.

As we already observed, God created man out of dust, which is where we get the name Adam, because it is the Hebrew word for "man" and also sounds like the Hebrew word for ground (Adamah). But why did God take Adam's rib to create Eve? Scripture does not say; however, in looking at the placement and purpose of the rib, perhaps it is symbolic.

Scripture says God took one of the man's ribs, a part of his side, and created Eve. This is important as we look at our roles as male and female. Just as the designated persons of the Triune are equally God with different responsibilities, man and woman are equally created, each having different responsibilities. The bone, or rib, that was taken from the side of man can symbolize how man and woman are equal.

It is interesting that woman originally came from man, and from then on, mankind has come from women. Even though God created man to be in relationship with Him, man is not equal to God, just as man is above and not equal to the animals. Man needed a companion that he could relate to and share life with in similar ways. What Adam needed was a suitable helper and God provided one. Adam and Eve are both equally responsible to care for God's creation, both equally loved by God, but both uniquely made to complement each other as a reminder that they need each other.

Let's first look at Adam. His rib was used to create Eve and I think that has significant meaning. The ribs are what protect the vital organs: they are strong and they are flexible. God created men with the ability to react quickly, and not hesitate from an emotional decision.

Men are better than women in wartime due to this ability. Even today where we have men and women on the battlefield, there are challenges that must be overcome. A woman's instinct is to hesitate from, let's say, shooting a child with a bomb due to her emotion affecting her decision-making, whereas a man (not diminishing the hardship of the task) will not hesitate, because his instinct is that if he hesitates it could result in multiple lives lost.

Men can separate emotion from the task at hand. Women must go through rigorous training to help minimize this hesitation, though it can never fully change because it is in her design, in her DNA, to have these emotional pulls. And it is a good thing.

Likewise, a man's instinct is to protect a woman; and having them on the battlefield creates a challenge, because he may get distracted and concerned over her safety and shift focus from the task at hand. I have even experienced this in the sports setting. When the women's rugby team I played on scrimmaged against the guys, the guys would not play as aggressively, because they knew they were stronger and could seriously hurt us.

This was not meant to be taken as offensive, but rather as a respect towards their female counterparts. Man's design is to protect and they are given more mental and physical strength to do just that.

I know we can all pick that one man that a woman can beat in a fight. There are those exceptions; however, the strongest man will always win against the strongest woman. But really, is it supposed to be a competition? That perspective is more likely due to our own insecurities and certain parts of society jumping in and ruffling the gender inequality feathers, than it is God getting glory for how He uniquely made us.

Men, when embracing how God created them, are warriors at heart. They seek to conquer (not to be mistaken with *lording over*) and they desire to protect their women counterpart. The first man, Adam, says it best when he declares: woman is "bone of my bone and flesh of my flesh." It becomes clear the view that Adam held towards woman. He is saying that she is a part of him and that just as he would take care of himself, he will take care of her. Just as parents are protective of their children who are "of their flesh," whether literally in the biological sense, adopted or blended family, men by design are protective of women.

Women are the help mate. Now, before we picture an early century housewife, slaving away doing chores and submitting to every command of the husband, you need to know what "helper" or "help mate" means. The same word is used in describing Jesus. It literally means "life line," or "to rescue."

Think about it: if a rib symbolizes the role of a man as protector, the heart would then be the symbol for the woman. She is the heart, the life line, the very thing that breathes life into her relationship with mankind.

When a woman is not in line with her design, she can become very bitter, mean, and spiteful, which will emotionally destroy life. Women are nurturers; compassionate and caring. When a child scrapes his knee, he tends to run to his mother for comfort because of her tender and nurturing heart. She not only physically tends to the injury, but emotionally encourages and tends to his well being.

When a professional sports player has the camera in his face, he tends to acknowledge his mom, typically because of the encouragement and support she has given. Much to the surprise of the father who may have spent hours throwing a football or practicing the fundamentals, it is the mother who gets the credit.

Again, I know we can pick out those men who are more nurturing or encouraging than some women, and yes, we all share similar character and personality traits of care, just as we do with protecting. But when it comes to the core and heart of a woman, it is in her design to love, just as Jesus loves and cares for His people.

God gets the glory when His creation lives out how He created us, rather than us abusing and perverting His design, especially when we complain that "it's not fair." That statement devalues how God uniquely created you, and you miss out on great opportunities to be alive in your design.

One aspect of how our design plays out in complementary roles is that God gives life, then equips males to protect life and equips females sustain life. It is a privilege that God allows us to have such great responsibility. It is sad when people abuse these roles and when sin perverts what was meant to be a pure, perfect, and beautiful cohesion.

God created man and woman to work together. Our talents, gifts, and roles are to complement and complete each other as God designed us. Just as the Trinity functions in perfection together, when man and woman are focused on God and sacrificially serve each other in their unique roles, God is glorified.

Wayne Grudem says it this way:

> *"The only distinctions between the members of the Trinity are in the ways they relate to each other and to the creation."*

Similarly, the distinctions between man and woman are in the ways they relate to each other and God in accordance to how they are designed. When either man or woman tries to step into God's role, the other's role, or choose not to act on what he or she is responsible for (as we will later see), heartache, hardship, and a break in the relationship between man and woman, and most importantly, between that person and God, occurs.

LIVING IN OUR DESIGN

By looking at the persons of the Trinity we can see how each are distinct beings with different roles.

God the Father is supreme in authority. He is the ultimate Judge who is responsible for devising a grand plan for all of creation and setting His will in motion. Nothing happens without the approval of the Father.

Jesus, God the Son, is responsible for carrying out the will of the Father and bringing Him glory. Jesus submits to the Father knowing that He has an ultimate plan. Jesus portrays God's humility, perfection, compassion, and God's grace and mercy. It is only through Jesus that we are no longer bound to the sinful nature of man, renewed and sanctified, inheriting our place with God in heaven.

The Holy Spirit is many times considered as our Guide. Some people consider Him as our conscience; but He is more than our inner thoughts that make up our conscience. The Holy Spirit is the Spirit of God who convicts us of wrong, gives discernment, reveals the will of God, and gives us wisdom and truth.

In the Gospel of John, Jesus talks about the Holy Spirit as our counselor, comforter, helper and guide. Once we choose to believe in Jesus as our Lord and Savior, the Holy Spirit comes to live in us.

He is our assurance of eternal security. A neat way to think of it is, once we have the Holy Spirit in us, every time God looks upon us, He sees a glimpse of himself. This makes sense, because He made us in His image and He is dwelling in us. It is important to acknowledge how each of the persons of the Trinity took a role in creation according to their attributes.

God the Father initiated creation and spoke it into existence as we read in Genesis 1:26. God the Son is whom creation came through, and in whom the plans of the Father are carried out. John 1:3 states,

> *"Through him all things were made; without him nothing was made that has been made"*

and in Colossians 1:16,

> *"For in him all things were created: things in heaven and on earth, visible and invisible, whether thrones or powers or rulers or authorities; all things have been created through him and for him.""*

The Spirit was what breathed life into creation and thus completed creation of man.

> *"The spirit of God has made me, and the breath of the Almighty gives me life."*

Job 33:4

The Spirit sustains and manifests God's immediate presence in His creation. In relation to how the roles of the Trinity contribute to our salvation, the Father designed and orchestrated how mankind would be redeemed (Galatians 4:4-5), Jesus carried out the plan of the Father (John 6:37-38), and the Holy Spirit draws us toward God's saving grace and transforms our lives (John 14:26, John 16:8; Romans

1:19-20). The Father, Son, and Spirit are equal in their divine attributes and each relate to mankind in a different way according to their specific role.

Headship and Submission

Just as the persons of the Trinity each has their own role, God also gave man roles and responsibility. We can start with Genesis 5:1-2:

> *"When God created man, he made them in the likeness of God. He created them male and female and blessed them. And he named them "man" when they were created."*

God was the first to name man, as in *Adam*, and then created man, as in *mankind*. God specifically chose a name that would apply to the entire human race. God gave *Adam* the responsibility to name the rest of creation, including woman. This can suggest that from the beginning of creation, God established a male leadership.

1 Corinthians 11:11-12 says;

> *"In the Lord, however, woman is not independent of man, nor is man independent of woman. For as woman came from man, so also man is born of woman. But everything comes from God."*

This headship can be seen first with Christ as stated in Colossians 1:15-20:

> *"The Son is the image of the invisible God, the firstborn over all creation. For in Him all things were created: things in heaven and on earth, visible and invisible, whether thrones or powers or rulers or authorities; all things have been created through Him and for Him. He*

> *is before all things, and in Him all things hold together. And He is the head of the body, the church; He is the beginning and the firstborn from among the dead, so that in everything He might have the supremacy. For God was pleased to have all His fullness dwell in Him, and through Him to reconcile to Himself all things, whether things on earth or things in heaven, by making peace through His blood, shed on the cross."*

We are reminded from this passage how we are created (in His image), why we are created (for Him), and His role (to reconcile us back to Him). In Ephesians 5:21-33, we see how the role of Christ mirrors our roles and design.

> *"Submit to one another out of reverence for Christ.*
> *Wives, submit yourselves to your own husbands as you do to the Lord. For the husband is the head of the wife as Christ is the head of the church, His body, of which He is the Savior. Now as the church submits to Christ, so also wives should submit to their husbands in everything.*
> *Husbands, love your wives, just as Christ loved the church and gave Himself up for her to make her holy, cleansing her by the washing with water through the word, and to present her to Himself as a radiant church, without stain or wrinkle or any other blemish, but holy and blameless. In this same way, husbands ought to love their wives as their own bodies.*
> *He who loves his wife loves himself. After all, no one ever hated their own body, but they feed and care for their body, just as Christ does the church—for we are members of his body. 'For this reason a man will leave his father and mother and be united to his wife, and the two will become one flesh.'*
> *This is a profound mystery—but I am talking about*

Christ and the church. However, each one of you also must love his wife as he loves himself, and the wife must respect her husband."

Before breaking this chapter down into gender specific roles, it's important to start with the shared role which is stated in the first sentence: "Submit to one another out of reverence to Christ." The First word we notice is the word "submit." This word is a verb, and not just any verb, but one that takes on its very definition to take action, show relation between two things, and is inflected through tone, voice, or mood. To submit is to yield to the power or authority of another, to allow yourself to be subjected to some kind of treatment, and to defer to another's judgment, opinion, decision, etc.

The second thing to look at is, we are to submit to one another. This again shows how we are created in equal value as man and woman. When we are living out God's design, we have total trust, respect, and pure belief of good intentions, motives, and care for the other person's well being.

This leads us to the third part of this sentence, which is submitting out of reverence of Christ. In order to understand this submission better, we need to look at a few more passages.

In John 4:34, Jesus says;

> *"My food is to do the will of the him who sent me to finish his work."*

Jesus even models this in teaching us how to pray by stating in Matthew 6:9;

> *"'Our Father in heaven, hallowed be Your name, Your kingdom come, Your will be done on earth as it is in heaven."*

In John 17:4, Jesus says;

> *"I have brought You glory on earth by completing the work You gave me to do."*

And in John 19:30, Jesus said;

> *"It is finished."*

With that, He bowed his head and gave up His spirit. These passages suggest that Jesus, though fully God, submitted to the will of the Father by carrying out His Father's plans. Likewise, we too must submit to God as our higher authority, but also to each other as having equal value and purpose.

We are to defer to each other's opinions and judgment, knowing God created us each with different perspectives and attributes. We are to treat each other with equal respect and extend care to one another and treat each other with the same love we want for ourselves.

As you read through the roles it is important to keep in mind that God created in perfection, and it was in perfection that these roles, responsibilities, and giftings sync together beautifully and flawlessly. Since sin has entered the picture, living in our design is difficult as selfishness, pride, abuse of roles, and distrust has perverted how God intends and desires the relational dynamic to be.

We should strive to live to the fullest within our design, and to do so we must be able to look at it through the lens God originally designed. We must also understand that how it plays out today is flawed; but that is no excuse to abandon, reject, or fail to live out our roles and design in which we are created. Just as there is a headship among God the Father and God the Son, there is headship between Jesus and the church.

> *"But I want you to realize that the head of every man is Christ, and the head of the woman is man, and the head of Christ is God."*
>
> 1 Corinthians 11:3

Ephesians 1:22 also states;

> *"And God placed all things under his feet and appointed him to be head over everything for the church."*

The church is made up of all the believers, and they have appointed leaders to help direct them. The church is to submit to Christ and follow His example of living out our true design. As believers, we submit ourselves to the church leadership and trust their judgment and teachings of scripture.

The final breakdown of headship we see is between men and women. As we know, nothing gets accomplished when there are two chiefs in one camp. When we look deeper into scripture we find that though there is equality, indeed, there is headship ascribed to man.

Even though we find this headship mentioned in the passages above, it actually started with creation in that woman was made from man. God did not create both at the same time: He created man first, then from man He made woman. Though they are created equal, their roles are different. Man was given the attribute from God the Father as being the head of woman, his wife; and this role was then extended to being head of the family when God told them to be fruitful and multiply.

In addition, woman was given the attribute of God the Son in that she gives life by bearing mankind, and as previously stated, she can encourage and sustain life emotionally. Even though man is head over woman, this does not mean he is more supreme; it just means God gave him a leadership role that is different from woman, and with this leadership role comes extra responsibilities that God places on man.

In a marriage, the husband is accountable for his wife. Both are accountable to each other and ultimately to God; however, because God specifically gave man the responsibility to lead his wife (and family) in obedience to God and His words; he bears the consequences of a failure to do so.

I know many husbands who have lost a sense of self and are being run over and controlled by their wives. And I know many wives who are exhausted from leading, feel alone, and are crying out for their husbands to step up. I believe the root of this is fear—fear from the wife to allow the husband to lead and thus relinquish the security of control; and fear from the husband to take the lead and risk failure or disappointing his wife/family.

This does not mean a woman cannot lead; quite the contrary. If we look in scripture we will see many instances where a woman led a nation (Deborah in Judges), instilled Godly wisdom (King Lemur's mother in Proverbs), or in general were chosen by God for specific purposes (Esther). God absolutely uses women in leadership positions and wants women to spiritually lead others. The difference is that a man is held more accountable in how he leads his family than a wife, because that is the charge set upon him by God, starting with Adam in the garden.

Role of woman

Let's look at the role of women as stated in Ephesians 5:22:

> *"Wives, submit to your husbands as to the Lord."*

I have heard where many have replaced the word "submit" with "respect," and even I got caught in that trap because it sounded better and my flesh could tolerate that word better than the seemingly oppressive "S" word. But respect is only a small piece of it, and when we try to put feel-good language on scripture we minimize its meaning, and are only partially obedient, which is still disobedient.

We must remember that we are looking at the word "submit" through a distorted lens. As we saw in the above definitions of "submit," respect is a part of it, but like the word "love," there are many layers and depths to it that must also be recognized and lived out. To submit to your spouse, or any other authority, is to respect their position, to recognize their role, to value their opinion and trust their direction.

In the original design, where there was no sin or selfishness, this was natural and easy; but once sin entered the picture, trust was broken, and that sense of trust plays a large role in our willingness to submit. It's easy to trust our own motives and agenda, but all of us struggle when it comes to trusting another person.

Dr. Larry Crabb says that feminine submission has a relational component to it. A woman is open to receive that which serves God's purposes and is ready to give out what she has stored up. There is not an attitude that comes with it, but rather a trust that she is arranging herself with a higher purpose, the glory of God.

In this Ephesians passage, it says the wife is to submit to the husband as the church submits to Christ. This does not mean that the husband is Christ to the woman, but rather that a wife should submit to her husband as act of submission to the Lord. If a woman is not married, then it is submission to the Lord and trusting His plan for her life.

Jesus trusted the Father's plan though it meant physically dying an agonizing death. Jesus trusted the greater plan God had for creation and was obedient to the Father's will. Similarly, we should trust God and the vision of our spouse and believe his desire to protect and care for us.

In general, we are all to submit to those who are in authority over us: whether it's a boss, law enforcement, political ruler. We are to be obedient to their direction and power of position, unless it outright goes against God's word as stated in Romans 13. Many of us have a good reason to distrust the one in authority over us; however, we are still called to submit unless it goes against God's word or puts us in harm's way.

Saying "No" to something that goes against scripture. is submitting to God; however, our approach needs to be God-honoring and one that will lead people toward God. A good example would be Daniel when he refused to bow in worship to the king.

> *"Wives, in the same way submit yourselves to your own husbands so that, if any of them do not believe the word, they may be won over without words by the behavior of their wives, when they see the purity and reverence of your lives.*
>
> *Your beauty should not come from outward adornment, such as elaborate hairstyles and the wearing of gold jewelry or fine clothes.*
>
> *Rather, it should be that of your inner self, the unfading beauty of a gentle and quiet spirit, which is of great worth in God's sight.*
>
> *For this is the way the holy women of the past who put their hope in God used to adorn themselves. They submitted themselves to their own husbands, like Sarah, who obeyed Abraham and called him her lord. You are her daughters if you do what is right and do not give way to fear."*
>
> 1 Peter 3:1-6

In this passage, we again read about submission, and how it it is God honoring. Whether married or single, when we submit to the Lord, others will see His character through us. The rest of these verses describe such character. It is a character of inner beauty, strength, and confidence.

In this passage, we are given the example of Sarah and Abraham. To put it in context, Sarah overheard the Lord tell Abraham she would have a son and she laughed because she was old and maybe biologically not able to produce children, or maybe it had been a while since she and Abraham were intimate. The main point here is that for whatever reason, she was not able to have a child and the notion of such a thing was humorous to her.

Sure enough, by the next year, she did have a child. Sarah, though the task seemed impossible, opened herself up to trust God and her husband by submitting to the thought, the act, and the responsibility of having a child. We too must not cave into fear of the unknown, impossible, or seemingly difficult tasks set before us, and open ourselves to trust.

To expand more on this passage, we see beauty is more than outward appearance; it is the beauty of a quiet and gentle spirit. This does not mean women are to be passive, quiet, and only speak when spoken to. Quite the opposite. The word "meek" is defined by a gentle and quiet spirit and describes someone who does not want to fight or argue.

Moses and Jesus are good examples of people who were meek. It is a confidence of knowing nothing can destroy you and that you are not controlled by fear. Confidence is an attractive trait, and when we are confident in who we are according to God's word and we rest in the ability to trust Him to work in and through us, we can have a gentle and quiet spirit because we don't have to prove our worth and value or defend our character.

We can also have assurance that we don't need to control others out of fear of getting hurt because our security lies in the confidence of who God is. Due to living in a broken world, we know that we will get hurt by others; however, we know that our well-being lies with God the Father. This confidence allows us to submit without fear, just as Jesus did, because man does not have the power to destroy the purposes of God.

Dr. Larry Crabb puts it this way:

> *"A deeply feminine woman is so at rest in God's delight of her undamageable beauty that she invites others to enjoy the beauty of God by relating invitationally not controllingly, openly not guardedly, courageously not defensively; to encourage another to be consumed by God's beauty at any cost to herself."*

Having a quiet spirit means that we will not seek revenge, make someone pay, hold grudges, or be passive-aggressive towards them. It also means that we will not call out every infraction in our relationships or point out how they should live properly.

Several times in Proverbs we read that a quarrelsome wife (or woman in general) is like a constant dripping of a leaky roof in a rainstorm. I have had leaky faucets, and the sound of each drip in the calm and quiet of a peaceful night gets to be very annoying and irritating. In fact, I have gone through great efforts in the night to try to minimize or diminish the undesirable sound.

Proverbs says the same about the husband or man. It says it is better for him to live on the corner of the roof than to share the whole house (Proverbs 21:9), and better to live in a desert than with a quarrelsome and nagging wife (Proverbs 21:19).

That sounds harsh, but unfortunately true. Proverbs 26:21 says this:

> *"As charcoal to embers and as wood to fire, so is a quarrelsome person for kindling strife."*

A woman without a meek spirit will repel others from seeing the glory of God at work in her through her relationships. Scripture says the tongue can be poisonous like a viper, pierce like a sword, and crush the spirit.

But when we are living in our design, our tongue is like choice silver (Proverbs 10:20), bringing healing (Proverbs 12:18), and giving life (Proverbs 15:4).

Solomon writes about how desirable the tongue can be in Song of Songs 4:11:

> *"Your lips drop sweetness as the honeycomb, my bride; milk and honey are under your tongue. The fragrance of your garments is like the fragrance of Lebanon."*

True to our design, we women can bring life or death by our words (Proverbs 18:21), and can build up or destroy those we are in relationships with. We come alive in our purpose of bringing glory to God through our role of submission to the Lord and by having a quiet spirit, full of confidence, and a gentle spirit that gives peace instead of conflict. By doing this, no matter what our circumstances, we can carry out the Lord's will of drawing others to God by the inward beauty of God reflected in us.

> *"Don't have anything to do with foolish and stupid arguments, because you know they produce quarrels. And the Lord's servant must not be quarrelsome but must be kind to everyone, able to teach, not resentful. Opponents must be gently instructed, in the hope that God will grant them repentance leading them to a knowledge of the*

> *truth, and that they will come to their senses and escape from the trap of the devil, who has taken them captive to do his will."*
>
> 2 Timothy 2:23-26

Before I close out this section, I want to comment on the 1 Corinthians 14:34 passage where it says;

> *"women should remain silent in the churches. They are not allowed to speak, but must be in submission."*

This verse is widely taken out of context and even jokingly used to put down women and their ministerial role. First, let me affirm that women absolutely have a role in the church and it's not just working with children, as some only deem them qualified for. This letter was sent to the church in a time where the church was in chaos. Prophesying and tongues were spoken over top each other with little to no interpretation, women were being disruptive and voicing varying opinions and questions, members of the church were running things how each saw fit, the male leaders were not leading the members in an order of worship. It was very disorderly, chaotic, and spiritually damaging.

Paul's instructions on silence were to bring peace and order into the worship experience. His instruction was not just to women, but also to those prophesying and speaking in tongues—that if there is no interpreter, one should remain silent. In going back to the role of women, women are to facilitate a warm environment where there is peace; not cause dissention, stir the pot, or contribute to any other disruption that would prevent spiritual growth.

There is a book called, *Why not Women?* that I recommend reading for anyone struggling to understand a woman's leadership role in ministry and seeking to find their place in a "man's world."

Role of Man

> *"Husbands, love your wives, just as Christ loved the church and gave himself up for her to make her holy, cleansing her by the washing with water through the word, and to present her to Himself as a radiant church, without stain or wrinkle or any other blemish, but holy and blameless.*
>
> *In this same way, husbands ought to love their wives as their own bodies. He who loves his wife loves himself."*
>
> Ephesians 5:25-28

The first thing we see in this passage is for husbands to love as Christ loved. How did Christ love the church? He died for her. A husband should be willing to die for his wife, and many men in their protective design would die for a child or a woman.

If we look in Colossians 3:19, we read that a husband is to love his wife and not be harsh. In the culture when this was written, wives were like property to their husbands. Paul was telling husbands to treat their wives with dignity and care, to cherish and honor them. Paul also wrote in 1 Corinthians 13: 4-6 (ESV) that,

> *"Love is patient and kind; love does not envy or boast; it is not arrogant or rude. It does not insist on its own way; it is not irritable or resentful."*

It is interesting how Ephesians 5:31 restates what God said in Genesis 2:24 after creating man and woman, that,

> *"for this reason a man will leave his father and mother and be united to his wife, and they will become one flesh."*

Since the husband and wife are one flesh, for the man to love his wife is to love the person who has become part of himself. That treatment is one of respect, worth, value, and equal importance.

For a man to love as Christ loves is to give himself up for her. In other words, sacrifice for her. But what does this sacrifice look like? Jesus' sacrifice was literally laying down His life. In the protective role, there are men who have done this for another person. While this is a brave and honorable act, sometimes sacrificially living for someone can be even harder. It can be a sacrifice of dreams, desires, career, pursuit of women, time, or something else. It is to put her first in all things and to lead her. He must take initiative to lead her and not become passive in his role.

To clarify on passivity, there are many men who are quiet leaders, who are not up front and center of a crowd, and yet still have strong leadership qualities. Those are men who do not mind others making general decisions, but who step up and are assertive when the time calls for it. The type of passivity I'm referring to is either being completely withdrawn and removed from their role, or becoming a doormat to their role. An example may be the man who is relying on the pastor of his church to lead his family rather than he himself leading his family, or even a situation in which the wife is dragging the family to church rather than the man leading his family to church.

Another example would be those men who are very vocal and out front in their leading. They must watch that they don't become prideful and put focus on self rather than Christ. Some men even fall guilty of being active in leading others, yet neglect or misread the spiritual barometer in their own family.

Humility in leading is important as a man should be willing to give credit away and take responsibility for failure or blame. This is hard for a man because it hits at his fears of inadequacy and failure. The good news is that in his weakness, God shows up and gets glory.

As man leads, he is directing and building others in a relationship with God. Christ did this by meeting people's physical needs first, though always keeping focus on the spiritual well-being. This means a husband needs to listen to his wife, be attentive to understanding her needs, bring her security and reassurance of those needs, and then direct her inward to her relationship with God. As a praying husband or father, his prayer life is not just owning his own sin, but also her sins and his children's sins by petitioning them on their behalf to the Lord, as Christ petitions them on our behalf to God the Father.

Timothy prays in 1 Thessalonians 3:13 for God to,

> *"strengthen [our] hearts so that [we] will be blameless and holy in the presence of our God and Father when our Lord Jesus comes with all his holy ones."*

This same strengthening is one which man must do for his family. He must tend to, protect, nurture, and grow her heart and sometimes the strengthening comes through correcting, challenging, and leading her out of her comfort zone.

A man who leads his wife recognizes her giftings, talents, and abilities and is not threatened by them, but builds her up in them. He does not take lightly her role as woman, see her as second class, a personal genie or servant. He treasures her giftings, input, and unique perspective. He values her opinions, thoughts and dreams, and takes them into consideration.

A woman being led by her husband is not intimidated by his role, nor does she mock his abilities. Instead, she respects him, trusts in his decision-making and values his leadership; even when she doesn't understand or disagrees.

A woman is not marrying her father, brother, or pastor. Her husband is unique in his leadership abilities, and though it may not be what she grew up with or admires in someone else, it does not mean he is inadequate, incapable, or incompetent. It also does not mean he is spiritually lacking.

It is wrong to compare him and measure his spiritual depthness based on her preferences or familiarity. God may very well be using those differences to challenge her in areas she needs and doesn't realize.

God is not a one-size-fits-all, and His creations aren't either. Embrace, admire, and build up the leadership skills your man has. If he is in a rut, not following God, or for whatever reason not leading the way he is designed to, don't lose hope in the man, or leader he can become, the one God designed him to be. Set your eyes on God as the ultimate leader and walk in your design; encouraging, supporting, and building him up as the man you believe he can be, the man God uniquely created him to be.

A COMPLEMENTARY RELATIONSHIP

God specifically told Adam he is to tend to the garden and work it. Adam is to also care for all creation and woman is responsible to help man in that role. Genesis 1:28-30 says,

> *"God blessed them and said to them, 'Be fruitful and increase in number; fill the earth and subdue it. Rule over the fish in the sea and the birds in the sky and over every living creature that moves on the ground.' Then God said, 'I give you every seed-bearing plant on the face of the whole earth and every tree that has fruit with seed in it. They will be yours for food. And to all the beasts of the earth and all the birds in the sky and all the creatures that move along the ground—everything that has the*

*breath of life in it—I give every green plant for food.'
And it was so."*

James says we are to look after the widows and orphans. Just as God provides for his people, man is to work to the best of his ability to provide for his family and help those who are not able to provide for themselves.

This does not necessarily mean the man must be the breadwinner, though the majority of men feel that need. Ultimately it is man's responsibility to work and God's responsibility to provide. Man is to give his wife that which she needs to live effectively in her design, and man is to help prepare his wife to live out her design so that she can glorify God and be holy and pleasing in His sight.

God truly designed man and woman to be complementary of each other. This does not mean that one who is not married is lacking, it just shows that when we have representation of both genders—whether in a job, ministry, church, marriage, or friendship—there is a well-rounded representation of our unique design that comes into play.

In relation to Jesus, this verse provides a good reflection as to how marriage reflects the relationship of Christ and the church. Today's society has perverted and twisted the godly roles designed specifically by God and assigned to us as mankind, us as a specific gender, and us as unique individuals with gifts and talents given by God. The design and role is seamless in practice when there is no sin; however, since we have been morally compromised, these roles can be taken advantage of.

Not every man treats a woman as precious as his own body, and in some situations, how he treats his own body is not how a woman would want to be treated. Women may experience fear, power trips, abuse, or be taken advantage of. On the other side, a woman may not respect, encourage, and build up a man. She may crush his spirit, or drive him to his downfall.

It is important to note that submitting is not always saying "Yes," and sacrificing doesn't mean being a doormat. Because of our sin and the brokenness of this world, we must have boundaries. We must choose a spouse or friends who are in align with the Spirit of God.

It is truly difficult on this earth to live out the design in which God originally made us. God wants man and woman to connect, but as we see from the opposite and unique design in which He created us, it is impossible to do so without our surrender to the workings of the Spirit. When we are able to see our design through the lens in which God created us, and when we rely on the guidance and help of the Holy Spirit, we can see our value, worth, and uniqueness and live out our roles as God intended.

IN NEED OF A SAVIOR

So where did things go wrong? If Adam and Eve were living a life of perfection in the garden, how did sin enter the picture? The first thing to know is that sin was already present. Not in the hearts of man at this time, but it was in the world. Somewhere between Genesis 1:31 where God saw all he created and said it was good, and Genesis 3:1 where the serpent deceived Eve, was a great angelic rebellion.

The original sin started with Lucifer, the most beautiful angel God created, who decided he wanted to be a god. He gathered some other angels who also did not like their position and rebelled. God, being a loving and merciful God, cast them out of heaven and allowed them to live on earth until Judgment Day.

God is a righteous God and He is a God who allows His creation to make moral choices. God is heartbroken when His creations make choices that are against His designs and purposes for them. But no matter how many bad choices His creations make or how far down that road of destruction they go, He still loves them.

But there are consequences. God tolerates sin for a time (as we know, based on his allowing of things here on earth), but God will not accept sin (as we know, based on his word regarding Judgment Day). There is a huge difference between those two concepts.

> *"Now the Lord God had planted a garden in the east, in Eden; and there he put the man he had formed. The Lord*

> *God made all kinds of trees grow out of the ground—trees that were pleasing to the eye and good for food. In the middle of the garden were the tree of life and the tree of the knowledge of good and evil.*
>
> *The Lord God took the man and put him in the Garden of Eden to work it and take care of it. And the Lord God commanded the man, 'You are free to eat from any tree in the garden; but you must not eat from the tree of the knowledge of good and evil, for when you eat from it you will certainly die.'*
>
> Genesis 2:8-9, 15-17

It may appear to some that God set Adam and Eve up. Why create a tree and put it where they may be tempted? Also, if God knew from the beginning what would happen, why not just bypass creating Lucifer (whom many believe to be Satan) or the tree?

As stated above, God gives us moral choice. He has predestined us for a great purpose and desires us to respond to His pursuits and choose Him. God desires us to be obedient and to follow His commands. Just as the angels had a choice during the angelic rebellion, man was also given a moral choice.

There are two trees mentioned in the garden, the tree of life which gives eternal life, and the tree of the knowledge of good and evil, which leads to death of those who eat it. Unknown to Adam, this death was a spiritual death of eternal separation from God. It is also a physical death in that man's physical design will fade away and die.

Adam and Eve possessed both life and moral discernment, as those attirbutes came from God. Their ability to eat from the tree of life shows that God's will was for them to have eternal life; however, by eating from the tree of the knowledge of good and evil, they were now operating out of a moral independence from God.

We will look at the events of Adam and Eve's Fall in Genesis 3 by breaking down each verse. This will give a better picture as to what took place. There is far more to the story than a snake convincing woman to eat a fruit and thus starting the downfall of man through sin.

> *"Now the serpent was more crafty than any of the wild animals the Lord God had made. He said to the woman, "Did God really say, 'You must not eat from any tree in the garden?'"*

Genesis 3:1

The serpent is none other than Satan. He was cast from heaven and given authority to freely roam the earth and is known as the prince of this world. Satan is more crafty than the animals, because he was not created as an animal, but was actually a great and majestic angel. We will discuss more on Satan later, but for now it is important to understand the he has an agenda and it opposes God.

He approached unsuspecting Eve and twisted around God's words found in Genesis 2:16 that states,

> *"You are free to eat from any tree in the garden."*

This took Eve's focus away from all the pleasing trees she was allowed to eat from, and shifted it to the only tree she was not allowed to eat from.

> *"The woman said to the serpent, 'We may eat fruit from the trees in the garden, but God did say, 'You must not eat fruit from the tree that is in the middle of the garden, and you must not touch it, or you will die.'"*

Genesis 3:2-3

God had actually told Adam in Genesis 2:17,

> *"but you must not eat from the tree of the knowledge of good and evil, for when you eat of it you will certainly die."*

Adam being the head of Eve relayed God's words to her. Eve knew what God had said, because Adam told her. Perhaps she thought Adam heard God wrong or didn't quite understand the situation, because Eve didn't just misquote what God had said, but she added to what God said in saying, *"… must not touch it."*

If we look through the Old Testament, we see where several people added to God's rules and laws, making it burdensome and very difficult to obey; and in some cases not even want to live for God. God has rules for our protection, and they are always with our best interest in mind. When man adds to those rules or commands, people start to question God's intentions for their lives.

So, here we are with Eve adding to God's word and playing into the deceiving hand of the serpent. Eve was starting to doubt what God had intended for them. Adam, being fully present for all of this, was not stepping up to correct Eve from her error or protect Eve from this serpent who was creating doubt. Adam was passive in his role. Perhaps he was curious and wondered what would happen. Maybe he didn't take God seriously regarding a consequence happening. We don't know why Adam didn't step up to his role; we just know that because he didn't, there was sin through his disobedience.

> *"'You will not certainly die,' the serpent said to the woman. 'For God knows that when you eat from it your eyes will be opened, and you will be like God, knowing good and evil.'"*
>
> Genesis 3:4-5

True to what Satan does today, he takes partial truths, and then distorts them, or lies outright. Adam and Eve will surely have a spiritual death upon eating the fruit and will also have a physical death, as we will later see. Satan blatantly denies a specific divine pronouncement. God said man would die if he ate from the tree of knowledge, and Satan told Eve she won't.

Satan creates a questioning, not just of God's word, but thinking that God is not trustworthy and is withholding something good from them. Satan even throws in his own sinful downfall by saying they *"will be like God"* through possessing this knowledge of good and evil.

Once again something is being narrowly focused in on, and Adam and Eve lose sight on all the ways God created them in his image. They are only seeing what they *thought* God was denying them. They don't stop to think *why* God may not have given them this ability from the start, and instead doubt God's goodness for them.

> *"When the woman saw that the fruit of the tree was good for food and pleasing to the eye, and also desirable for gaining wisdom, she took some and ate it. She also gave some to her husband, who was with her, and he ate it. Then the eyes of both of them were opened, and they realized they were naked; so they sewed fig leaves together and made coverings for themselves."*
>
> Genesis 3:6-7

Both Adam and Eve were caught up in doubt and curiosity. Previously this tree and its fruit did not capture their attention, look desirable, or was tempting to eat; but now that Eve has focused in on what she is being denied, the fruit looked very desirable, even more than the other fruits that were good for eating. It is interesting how the same tactics of the enemy that were used then are used now. The things that didn't previously hold our attention or curiosity, once pointed out, becomes something we can't get our focus off of. We become fixated on them. We are never tempted by bad or ugly things, as we would immediately say "No" and recognize the deception. We are tempted by the seemingly good things, the things we want, desire, or think we lack.

Eve took the fruit from the tree and bit into it while Adam watched. Again, Adam had an opportunity to step up and pull Eve away, tell her "No," or chase away this serpent. Instead Adam watched to see what would happen to Eve. When Adam saw that nothing seemingly happened to Eve when she took a bite—he ate some too. Instantly upon eating the fruit, their eyes were opened to evil. Adam and Eve chose to morally sin by disobeying God. Their perfection and purity was compromised, and in its place was shame.

Here were two people God had joined together as a couple, who had stood naked before each other from the moment He created them, and now there was shame and embarrassment over their nakedness. As a married couple, they should not have been ashamed to stand naked in front of each other, but their sin distorted their view of each other and self.

Even today the majority of people cannot stand naked by their own self (let alone with a spouse) in front of a mirror and appreciate and value how God created them without feeling ashamed, vulnerable, exposed, or insecure. Sin distorted our perception of what God created as good. Naked and ashamed, Adam and Eve sewed fig leaves to cover themselves in an attempt to hide their shame and gain a sense of security.

> *"Then the man and his wife heard the sound of the Lord God as he was walking in the garden in the cool of the day, and they hid from the Lord God among the trees of the garden. But the Lord God called to the man, 'Where are you?'"*
>
> Genesis 3:8-9

When they heard God, they hid out of fear and shame. The same God they used to walk with in the garden, and share everything with, they were now hiding from and fearful of. Still true today, shame and fear has been a tool of the enemy to keep us from turning to the only God who can redeem and restore. God, through his Spirit, convicts us of sin and sorrow. Guilt and shame can be a byproduct feeling of conviction, but God does not want us to live a life of shame and guilt.

God called out to Adam specifically as he was the most responsible in his headship position. God asked the question, *"Where are you?"* not because he didn't know where he was, but rather it was more of a rhetorical question of where he was spiritually. It was a heart issue question. God already knew what they had done and he knew the shame they felt. God also knew it was not good for man to be left in his sin; that man needed to confess and repent to break from the bondage of sin and shame.

> "He answered, 'I heard you in the garden, and I was afraid because I was naked; so I hid.' And he said, 'Who told you that you were naked? Have you eaten from the tree that I commanded you not to eat from?' The man said, 'The woman you put here with me—she gave me some fruit from the tree, and I ate it.'"
>
> Genesis 3:10-12

God gave Adam an opportunity to confess his sin. Rather than owning up to the sin and accepting responsibility and accountability for his actions, Adam put blame not just on the woman, but on God, since He created woman. That takes some guts to point the finger back at God. As a leader, Adam should have owned up to his failure in leading his wife and his failure to remain morally pure. Instead, Adam deflected his part in the sinful action and rejected the role God gave him.

> *Then the Lord God said to the woman, 'What is this*

> *you have done?' The woman said, 'The serpent deceived me, and I ate.'"*
>
> Genesis 3:13

God turned to woman and gave her the same opportunity to repent. Rather than owning up to her sin, Eve also deflected her own culpability by blaming the serpent. True to what humans do today, we deflect or deny our sin. We have an excuse, can seemingly justify, or can blame another of causing us to sin or even sinning worse than us to take the focus and conviction of us.

> *"So the Lord God said to the serpent, 'Because you have done this, 'Cursed are you above all livestock and all wild animals! You will crawl on your belly and you will eat dust all the days of your life. And I will put enmity between you and the woman, and between your offspring and hers; he will crush your head, and you will strike his heel.'"*
>
> Genesis 3:14-15

Because God is a just and holy God, there must be consequence for sin. Here we see that God cursed the serpent. Most scholars believe that the serpent walked upright, like a lizard, and then in the curse was forced to crawl on the belly. What a huge fall from being the most beautiful angel created in the heavenly realms to now being cast so low that he is crawling on his belly in dirt.

The antagonism between people and snakes is symbolic of the struggle between God and the evil one. There is foreshadowing here as Satan struck at God through the crucifixion of Jesus Christ; however, Christ crushed Satan by defeating him through the cross. Satan lashes out at mankind by destroying their relationships with each other and God; however, mankind has shared in the victory over Satan because of the cross, and on the day of Christ's return will share in the final victory over Satan and all evil powers for eternity.

> *"To the woman he said, 'I will make your pains in childbearing very severe; with painful labor you will give birth to children. Your desire will be for your husband, and he will rule over you.'"*
>
> Genesis 3:16

God does not curse man and woman; however, He does cast His judgment and they have consequences from their sin. God being the just God He is and a God of intention, gives woman a punishment in according to her design. The very things that He has given as a blessing to woman, the ability to reproduce man, will now become a painful experience. The consequence of her sin also plays out in her design and role. Rather than being an encourager and companion, she is in competition with man. Rather than freely trusting in her husband's leadership role and headship, she questions his ability to protect and care for her and uses control as a security method.

The fact that woman is still able to bear children shows the grace of God; however, the sexual and intimate relations between man and woman can be contentious rather than an absolute joy and blessing.

> *"To Adam he said, 'Because you listened to your wife and ate fruit from the tree about which I commanded you, You must not eat from it, Cursed is the ground because of you; through painful toil you will eat food from it all the days of your life. It will produce thorns and thistles for you, and you will eat the plants of the field. By the sweat of your brow you will eat your food until you return to the ground, since from it you were taken; for dust you are and to dust you will return.'"*
>
> Genesis 3:17-19

Adam also did not step up in his design to protect Eve and act according to his leadership role, especially since God specifically gave

Adam a command. It was his job to obey, and to also ensure Eve obeyed as well. Like the curse on the snake, God curses the ground from which He made Adam.

The ground will no longer be the perfect and fertile ground as in the garden, nor the vegetation prime for picking. There will now be thorns, weeds, thistles, and a soil that can be hard or lacking in nutrients needed for growth.

Notice again how God doesn't curse man or woman; however, like the judgment on Eve, God judged man in accordance to his design and role. Man would have to work long and hard to provide for his family. This means there is sweat, scrapes, cuts, calloused hands and feet, sore muscles, and fatigue. The grace God gives man through this is that he will still have the ability to provide food that sustains life. Where before food from the tree of life allowed them to physically live for eternity, Adam's labor will not be able to prevent physical death.

> *"Adam named his wife Eve, because she would become the mother of all the living."*
>
> Genesis 3:20

In Genesis 1:5, God created the light and darkness and called it day and night. In ancient Near East, for a king to name something was an act of claiming dominion over over it. God has dominion over the cosmic realms and all that lies within; however, God allowed humans to name the creatures they were given dominion over. In verse 20 above, Adam was not naming woman *Eve* out of dominion of her, but rather as a recognition of her and her role for the whole human race, including himself.

In Hebrew, "Eve" means "life." Adam was placing significance on Eve's role as a giver of life and valuing her as God intended him to.

> *"The Lord God made garments of skin for Adam and his wife and clothed them."*
>
> Genesis 3:21

God provided a better covering for Adam and Eve than their makeshift fig leaves. Man is not able to cover their sin and shame like God. For God to provide more efficient garments of skin for Adam and Eve, there was bloodshed. There had to have been a sacrifice of an innocent animal to have the skin covering. This first shedding of blood was done by God due to first man's sin.

As we see in the Old Testament, innocent animals were sacrificed to cover man's sins, so the relationship can be restored and man does not have to hide from God in fear and shame. There had to be innocent bloodshed as a covering for those sins. As promised and foretold, God the Father sent Jesus to cover our sin once and for all.

God the Father made the first sacrifice for man by killing some of His own creation; and God the Son made the final and ultimate sacrifice, by allowing Himself to be killed to cover man's sins and restore the broken relationship for eternity. We will discuss more on sacrifices in the next chapter.

> *"And the Lord God said, 'The man has now become like one of us, knowing good and evil. He must not be allowed to reach out his hand and take also from the tree of life and eat, and live forever.' So the Lord God banished him from the Garden of Eden to work the ground from which he had been taken.*
>
> *After He drove the man out, He placed on the east side of the Garden of Eden cherubim and a flaming sword flashing back and forth to guard the way to the tree of life."*
>
> Genesis 3:22-24

God banished Adam and Eve for their own protection, the same reason God gave commands for man to obey—for their own good and protection. The tree of life gave eternal life to man. Now that man's morality had been compromised, if man were allowed to continue to eat from the tree of life, he would be living eternally in total depravity. This is not good for man, nor what God desires for us and created us to be.

God had to protect man from themselves and so He kicked Adam and Eve out of the garden and guarded the way back in. The original sin began with Lucifer and his rebellion against God. Inherited sin started when Adam and Eve sinned, and from that point mankind was born as sinners, morally compromised, and depraved. God knew what would have to take place to restore mankind back to their original design, and man is again given the choice.

REDEEMED AND RESTORED
IN RIGHTEOUSNESS

Sin is the failure to abide in the moral law of God, whether through an act, attitude, thought, or some other way. Friendships, marriages, people, dreams, relationships all suffer because of sin. Matthew 15:19 says,

> *"For out of the heart come evil thoughts—murder, adultery, sexual immorality, theft, false testimony, slander."*

Due to our inherited sin, we are born into depravity, born into the moral corruption and wickedness of our flesh. It is hard to think this when you look at a new baby. We think innocence and purity; however, even a baby has inherited moral sin. We know this because God tells us and we can also attest to this because one does not have to teach a child selfishness. They are immediately selfish, saying "Mine!" They are self-centered, believing everything revolves around them, and interested only in how something impacts them, and their self-gratification.

No one is exempt from the condemnation of their sin. Romans 5:12 says,

> *"Therefore, just as sin entered the world through one man, and death through sin, and in this way death came to all people, because all sinned."*

For God to allow us, as corrupt beings, into eternity with Him would go against His nature, His very being. As stated previously, God *tolerates* sin for a time, but God cannot *accept* sin. God's righteousness demands a punishment for sin. God cannot just excuse it; there must be justice because that is the very nature of God and God cannot go against His nature and very existence.

That punishment is death, as declared by God in the garden before man sinned. Hell is where those who oppose God due to their spiritual corruption, such as Satan and the fallen angels (demons), are condemned to for eternity.

The good news is that even before the fall of man, there was hope—hope of an eternal life the way God originally desired it, life the way it was before sin. We know this because in looking back to the curse of the serpent, God said the serpent will be crushed by the offspring of man. God was going to bring someone who would destroy Satan and all evil.

Adam and Eve, and their offspring, did not know who this person would be, but their faith was in the word of God as they looked toward this savior. Hope on earth is due to God. We can have peace, calmness, strength and help in the midst of pain and circumstances because of confidence in who God is and what God has done on the cross.

There is no hope in hell. It is final.

Moral corruption continued to spiral immediately after the fall of Adam and Eve. We see in Genesis 4 that Adam and Eve bore Cain and and Abel. Cain worked the land and Abel tended the flock. When bringing an offering to the Lord, Cain was angry and jealous of Abel's favor with God, perhaps because Abel brought the best portions of some of the firstborn of his flock, whereas Cain brought only some of the fruits of the soil.

God warned Cain in Genesis 4:7 and it is a warning to us all that,

> *"sin is crouching at your door, it desires to have you, but you must master it."*

This word "desire" is the same word used for Eve's judgment on *desiring* her husband, and in Song of Solomon 7:10 where the Lover talks about her husband *desiring* her. It is an all-consuming desire, waiting to possess, a desperation to have hold of. This warning unfortunately did not prevent Cain from murdering his brother.

God came to Cain, similarly to his experience with Adam in the Garden, and posed the rhetorical question, "Where is your brother Abel?" (Genesis 4:9) God again was getting to the heart issue, desiring man to confess and repent. Cain lied to God, and then sarcastically and callously replied, "Am I my brother's keeper?"

With this indifference and lack of moral conviction on top of the original sin of murder, God cursed Cain, saying the ground would no longer produce food for him and that he would be a restless wanderer. Cain went out from the Lord's presence.

Again, this shows how God does not accept sin and there is punishment for sin. However, God marked Cain and said that no man was allowed to kill him. Even amid sin, God gives grace and mercy, and has a plan and purpose for man. Grace is giving someone something he does not deserve, and mercy is not giving someone what he does deserve.

Sin continued to spiral in mankind to the point where:

> *"The Lord saw how great man's wickedness on the earth had become, and that every inclination of the thoughts of his heart was only evil all the time. The Lord was grieved*

> *that He had made man on the earth, and His heart was filled with pain. So the Lord said, 'I will wipe mankind, whom I have created, from the face of the earth—men and animals, and creatures that move along the ground, and the birds of the air—for I am grieved that I have made them.'*
>
> Genesis 6:5-7

The fact that man's heart was evil all the time showed man's total depravity. Mankind had stopped looking towards a restored relationship with God and lacked the desire to do right in the eyes of the Lord. They were now living for their own selfish desires. The sin of humans created sorrow with God and God would pour out His judgment on the world, including the innocent animals, because they were under the rule of man.

Genesis 6:8-9 says that Noah was a righteous man and found favor with the Lord because he walked with God and sought after Him. God decided to flood the world, but would spare Noah and his family. Noah built an ark as God specified and his family, along with two of every unclean animal and seven of every clean animal (for sacrificial offerings and later for food), lived in the ark until God's judgment on the world was complete.

After Noah, his family, and all the animals and creatures came out of the ark, Noah built an altar to the Lord, took some of all the clean animals and clean birds, and sacrificed burnt offerings on it.

> *"The Lord smelled the pleasing aroma and said in his heart: 'Never again will I curse the ground because of humans, even though every inclination of the human heart is evil from childhood. And never again will I destroy all living creatures, as I have done.'"*
>
> Genesis 8:21

Redeemed and restored in righteousness

"Then God blessed Noah and his sons, saying to them, 'Be fruitful and increase in number and fill the earth. The fear and dread of you will fall on all the beasts of the earth, and on all the birds in the sky, on every creature that moves along the ground, and on all the fish in the sea; they are given into your hands. Everything that lives and moves about will be food for you. Just as I gave you the green plants, I now give you everything. Man's diet now includes meat, however God values life and makes it clear that it is blood that gives life and that man is not to get involved in pagan rituals where bloodlife is sought out as a source of power or preservation of life.

'But you must not eat meat that has its lifeblood still in it. And for your lifeblood I will surely demand an accounting. I will demand an accounting from every animal. And from each human being, too, I will demand an accounting for the life of another human being.

'Whoever sheds human blood, by humans shall their blood be shed; for in the image of God has God made mankind.

'As for you, be fruitful and increase in number; multiply on the earth and increase upon it.'

Then God said to Noah and to his sons with him: 'I now establish my covenant with you and with your descendants after you and with every living creature that was with you—the birds, the livestock and all the wild animals, all those that came out of the ark with you—every living creature on earth. I establish my covenant with you: Never again will all life be destroyed by the waters of a flood; never again will there be a flood to destroy the earth.'"

Genesis 9:1-11

When Noah gave a sacrifice of worship to God, we are told it was a pleasing aroma to God. God took delight in the offering and made a covenant with Noah. God renewed His original provision for man's food and added to it meat from some animals.

God is very clear about blood and how it gives life. God made us in His image and is a defender of human life because we are His creation and because we represent Him. God established a covenanted assurance that He will not destroy earth and its inhabitants until His purposes for creation are realized in redemption.

In looking through the Old Testament, we see how people used sacrificial offerings as an act of worship from the first of their crops, to poured offerings, to the best choice of their animals. In Leviticus, animal sacrifice was given as an atonement for the sins of the Israelites—either individually or collectively as a nation. The bloodshed was to cover the wrongs they have done so that God would forgive them.

After Moses comes down from Mount Sinai, we see the Law come into play. There were different animal sacrifices for each sin, and God's laws of how to go about the sacrifice had to be observed and honored to the very detail. The law was given so that man would know how to live and how to temporarily restore the broken relationship with God until the day God would send the One who would save man from their sin.

Ultimate love sacrifice

Just as God cast Adam and Eve into the wilderness, Jesus came to the wilderness. He meets us where we are. All throughout Jesus' ministry, the Bible gives us examples of how He met people where they were. The poor, the disabled, the broken, the adulterer, the prideful, the greedy, the hopeless, the condemned; He met them with love and compassion, oftentimes meeting their physical needs first before correcting and leading them to spiritual repentance and freedom. Jesus brings us hope—the hope of a reconciled relationship with God.

God loves not because of who we are, but because of who He is. We cannot do anything to make God love us more, nor can we do anything to make God love us less. John 15:13 says this:

> *"Greater love has no one than this: to lay down one's life for one's friends."*

John 3:16 says,

> *"For God so loved the world that He gave His one and only Son, that whoever believes in Him shall not perish but have eternal life."*

And 2 Corinthians 5:21 says,

> *"God made Him who had no sin to be sin for us, so that in Him we might become the righteousness of God."*

God loves us so much that He was willing to come as a weak and vulnerable baby, to be raised by teenagers who were poor, to grow up experiencing the hardships of life, and to accept a torturous death He did not deserve, because of the sinful pride and insecurity of man. He, being fully God, became fully man in order to redeem us into a righteous relationship with Him.

His blood was the final and ultimate sacrifice that restored and secured our eternal life with God. The animal sacrifices were necessary, but temporary; Jesus' death-sacrifice was permanent, and covered past, present, and future sins.

Unlike the fallen angels, God, in His love, chose to spare mankind.

Once God decided to save man, there was no other way to do so without the blood of Jesus. Atonement for sin was a necessary consequence of the Father's decision to save mankind.

Before Jesus was arrested and killed, He prayed three times for God to take the cup from Him, but then He said for God the Father's will, rather than His own, to be done (submission to the Father). Again, this shows that it was not possible for Jesus to avoid the death consequence for sin, for man to be accepted back into eternal relationship with God.

Jesus was in so much agony over what would take place that He was sweating blood, literally. The intense amount of distress Jesus was in caused his blood vessels to constrict to the point of rupture. Jesus was not in agony due to the physical pain He would endure, but rather the spiritual separation He would have from the Father.

Hell is complete separation from God and Jesus knew that by taking on the sins of the world past, present, and future, He would temporarily suffer in his relationship with God the Father. Jesus willingly put Himself into this agony, before his enemies gave him any trouble, to show that He was offering Himself out of free will; that His life was not forced from Him. He laid it down Himself. John 10:18 says,

> *"No one takes it from me, but I lay it down of my own accord. I have authority to lay it down and authority to take it up again. This command I received from my Father."*

We are still living in judgment of sin; however, by choosing to believe in Jesus, His death, and resurrection, all our sins past, present, and future, have been forgiven. Jesus' blood covers our sins. His bloodshed and sacrifice fulfilled the law. Jesus says in Matthew 5:17,

> *"Do not think that I have come to abolish the Law or the Prophets; I have not come to abolish them but to fulfill them."*

The law was put in place so that people knew how to cover their sins and renew their heart. The law was also put in place for people's protection and health. Many took the law (or the word of God) and added to it, making things more taxing. I think men added to God's laws for extra assurance. It may have started from a good motive, but it got taken to the extreme and man's laws became confused with God's laws.

There is not a ledger system at work. We can never "do" enough good to cover our sin and earn our way into heaven. God is a God of freedom. Man's laws are restrictive, whereas God's laws are freeing and for our benefit. The law was necessary as it was man's way to cover sin in accordance to what God established. But the law never did nor ever will save us—that is legalism. The laws and sacrifices were more for our sake and heart conviction. It was a temporary measure until Jesus fulfilled the law by his death on the cross. Romans 3:20 says,

> *"Therefore no one will be declared righteous in God's sight by the works of the law; rather, through the law we become conscious of our sin."*

Romans 3:21-26 says:

> *"But now apart from the law the righteousness of God has been made known, to which the Law and the Prophets testify. This righteousness is given through faith in Jesus Christ to all who believe. There is no difference between Jew and Gentile, for all have sinned and fall short of the glory of God, and all are justified freely by his grace through the redemption that came by Christ Jesus.*

> *God presented Christ as a sacrifice of atonement, through the shedding of His blood—to be received by faith. He did this to demonstrate his righteousness, because in His forbearance He had left the sins committed beforehand unpunished—He did it to demonstrate His righteousness at the present time, so as to be just and the one who justifies those who have faith in Jesus."*

God has fixed the broken relationship for good, and it was by His hand and through His will, not man's. Even though Jesus fulfilled the law, this does not mean that we can do whatever we want now that our sins are forgiven. We still need to be obedient to God's word.

Obedience and disobedience are heart issues that can either grow our relationship or bring us down. Conviction is of God, through the Holy Spirit that now lives in those who believe. Conviction keeps us in line with God's word, leads us to repentance, and creates a right heart.

Unhealthy guilt and shame come from the enemy to keep us from running to God. It is toxic and can prevent us from fully functioning. Our conviction comes from the Spirit of God who lives in us once we surrender our will to God. This is the Spirit that brings peace and direction on how to live, which leads us to sanctification.

> *"'The word is near you; it is in your mouth and in your heart,' that is, the message concerning faith that we proclaim: If you declare with your mouth, Jesus is Lord and believe in your heart that God raised Him from the dead, you will be saved. For it is with your heart that you believe and are justified, and it is with your mouth that you profess your faith and are saved. As Scripture says, 'Anyone who believes in Him will never be put to shame.' For there is no difference between Jew and*

> *Gentile—the same Lord is Lord of all and richly blesses all who call on him, for, 'Everyone who calls on the name of the Lord will be saved.'"*
>
> Romans 10:8-13

Salvation is not just believing in Jesus, because even the demons know and believe in who Jesus is. It is about surrendering your life. It's surrendering your heart, mind, and soul to the One who made you. When we choose to accept Jesus as our ultimate sacrifice for sins, and surrender our lives to the Father's will, we are given the Holy Spirit as a deposit guaranteeing our salvation. When God looks at us, He sees Himself. We are judged, but God sees his blood and righteousness and we are not condemned.

As we read in Romans 3, Jesus was an atoning sacrifice. Isaiah 53:10 says the Lord makes His life an offering for sin. Throughout the Old Testament, God says the sacrificial offerings were "a pleasing aroma." Jesus being the ultimate sacrifice is a pleasing aroma to God. His perfect and pure life was the only sacrifice that would cover all of mankind. It was God's sacrifice of self that was sufficient enough and strong enough to take on and bear the sins of all humanity; past, present, and future.

Only God could truly redeem His people from the bondage of sin and the death penalty for that sin. This is because only God, who created hell, could conquer hell and leave the sins of the world behind. Up until this point, sacrifices were temporary coverings that had to be done at different times. Jesus was the ultimate sacrifice. His blood purchased us back into a relationship with God for eternity. Unlike Abel's blood who cried out for vengeance, Jesus' blood was that of grace.

Jesus, who is the only being strong enough to bear it, took on the sins of all mankind. In doing so, Jesus fulfilled the need for sacrifice (someone to pay the penalty of death), propitiation (someone to take away the deserving wrath of God from us), reconciliation (someone to bring us back into relationship with God), and redemption (someone who can purchase us and free us from the bondage of sin).

Scripture says that after enduring much suffering and with the unfathomable burden of taking on mankind's sin, Jesus cried out to the Father saying, *"Eloi, Eloi, lema sabachthani?"* which means "My God, my God, why have You forsaken me?" (Mark 15:34). Jesus undertook the full wrath of God which was intended for man. Where since the beginning of eternity Jesus was in a divine relationship with God the Father, He was now at this moment in time no longer able to be in fellowship with the Father. In essence, Jesus was abandoned by the Lord. Remember, the Father cannot accept sin, and thus, even though Jesus is God, the sins of the world that Jesus took upon Himself cannot, in the very nature of God, reside with God. Thus, with a loud cry, Jesus gave up His spirit to the will of the Father and physically died.

The coming of Jesus our Lord and Savior to dwell on earth and give a willing death sacrifice was only the first part of salvation: His resurrection was the second part. We cannot have a resurrection without a death, and the death would not have served its full purpose without the resurrection.

The Apostle's Creed states that Jesus descended into hell and then rose again (conquering hell). However, the Creed was gradually developed over the span of 550 years, and the phrase was not found in the earlier development of the Creed. It is believed the real meaning of the phrase was that Christ was dead and buried in the grave. That Jesus descended into the grave, a physical death, not the spiritual death of hell where there was punishment and separation from God.

On the cross, as we saw above, Jesus felt the very separation from God the Father as he bore upon Himself all sin for all mankind and made Himself a sacrificial offering. When Jesus said, "it is finished," and committed His spirit to the Father, Jesus joined His Father in heaven, ending His suffering and estrangement from the Father. We know Jesus went to be with the Father because Jesus told the thief on the cross that,

> *"Today you will be with me in paradise."*
> Luke 23:43

Scripture indicates that because Jesus died on the cross, He fulfilled and completely satisfied the demands of the Father. His sacrifice was accepted and there was no more suffering that needed to take place. Because He is fully God, Jesus conquered death in that He physically rose again (resurrected) on the third day after His death. Jesus' resurrection was not just a coming back to life as Lazarus did, nor did Jesus have anyone resurrect Him: It was the authority He had been given by the Father to be able to do.

There was also no second death for Jesus, but rather a new life and renewed body such as we will experience one day in heaven. When we surrender our lives to Jesus, we have a new life spiritually; however, we do not have a renewed physical body yet. Our physical bodies are still subject to weakness, illness, and death until the day Jesus returns and we are given our perfect new bodies.

Jesus now mediates between God and man in the new covenant. Jesus, on our behalf, goes to the Father and offers up our prayers to Him. God the Father, through the redeeming blood of Jesus, hears Jesus' pleas for His people, and Jesus, being our mediator, carries to man the favors of the Father.

Just as Jesus pleads with God for us, He also pleads with us for God through the Spirit. There are those who believe that God as the Spirit is the relational being of the Father and Son. When Jesus left the earth to be with God in heaven, the Holy Spirit came down to dwell in those who believed and even now comes to dwell in those who choose to believe and surrender their lives to the will of the Father.

The power of the resurrection was more than just Jesus raising physically from the grave; it is also the power that has been given to those who believe. Ephesians 1:19-20 says it is an

> *"…incomparably great power for us who believe. That power is like the working of His mighty strength, which He exerted in Christ when He raised Him from the dead and seated Him at His right hand in the heavenly realms."*

This new resurrection power in us includes power over sin in our lives, power to endure hardships and power for ministry. It is the power we need to do the will of God while living in a broken world full of sin.

Even though we are a new creation and possess the Holy Spirit, we are still living in a broken world and have not yet been born again into our new bodies. Therefore, we still sin in our flesh. The Holy Spirit convicts us of sins. Even though Jesus died for our sins and they are forgiven, conviction and asking of forgiveness is a heart issue that allows the relationship with God to be restored—which is the same reason God asked Adam the rhetorical question, "where are you?"

The Holy Spirit gives us the peace and comfort that no matter what trials we are in or how bad we have messed up, God's will cannot be thwarted. The Spirit guides us on the plans of the Father and aligns our desires with God's will. God's will from the beginning was for man to have a relationship with Him for eternity.

Sin ruined the original plan; however, Jesus' blood allows there to be redemption and restoration for those who choose to accept it, and the

Spirit living in us is our guarantee that God has accepted the blood sacrifice of Himself through Jesus.

Salvation is a free gift from God that can never be taken away. Once you choose to accept it, no matter what mistakes you make, Jesus already paid the ultimate price to cover those sins and God has already granted acceptance of you into His Kingdom.

A Fragrant Offering

In Revelation 8 there is mention of an angel who has a golden censer (which is used to hold charcoal for burning of incense). The angel came and stood at the altar. It is believed this "other angel" is actually Jesus. It says:

> *"Another angel, who had a golden censer, came and stood at the altar. He was given much incense to offer, with the prayers of all God's people, on the golden altar in front of the throne. The smoke of the incense, together with the prayers of God's people, went up before God from the angel's hand. Then the angel took the censer, filled it with fire from the altar, and hurled it on the earth; and there came peals of thunder, rumblings, flashes of lightning and an earthquake."*
>
> Revelation 8:3-5

As we see here, the prayers of those who are in Christ never go unnoticed or unanswered. Jesus, on our behalf, interceded for us on the cross by taking our punishment, and continues to intercede for us by presenting our prayers, requests, and petitions before God the Father.

As we just read in scripture, these prayers that were accepted in heaven produced great changes upon earth. The same angel that in his censer offered up the prayers of the saints, in that same censer took of the fire of the altar and cast it into the earth. The events that followed covered both saints and sinners: answered prayers for the saints, and anger against the world which He would use to avenge Himself and His people. Jesus fulfilled the curse and promise of God from back in the Garden.

Satan and sin will be crushed and conquered for good, and cast into hell for all eternity. God is also leading towards fulfilling the judgment that man will be condemned to eternal death in hell, without hope and without access to God, except for the men who have surrendered their lives to the Lord, who will have redemption of eternal life with God with their resurrected and new body.

OUR VALUE, WORTH, AND PURPOSE

Adam looked to his Creator for validation and worth. Eve looked to Adam for direction (God's words), since it was Adam's responsibility to relay to her the things God shared with him, but she did not look to Adam for her worth and validation: she too looked to God as her creator.

Many times we lose sight of the one whose voice should be the loudest in affirming who we are, giving us purpose, and validating our identity. Too many times we look to man, woman, our job, title, or status to give us that validation of worth. The problem with that is; whoever or whatever we give the power to *validate* our identity also has the power to *invalidate* us. We should affirm each other regarding who we are because of Christ, and not put our worth and value of who we are in man or the things we obtain here on earth.

As we have read, after God created man, He said, "It is good." Even though sin has distorted things, we never lost the image of God in which He created us. Because of Christ, the fullness of that image is restored. David, known as a man after God's heart, sinned and messed up many times, yet he still praised God and believed that, despite his shame and insecurity, God still loved him and had plans for him.

> *"For you created my inmost being; you knit me together in my mother's womb. I praise you because I am fearfully*

> *and wonderfully made; your works are wonderful, I know that full well."*
>
> Psalm 139:13-14

From the very start of the union that creates life, God knew the egg and sperm that would pair to create you. Out of all the potential genetic combinations, God knew the traits, attributes, and person you would be. God orchestrated and designed you.

Luke says in his gospel that,

> *"...the very hairs on your head are all numbered."*
>
> Luke 12:7

God knows every detail of you, including some things that even you don't know. And it's not just the physical aspects of our bodies or the personality of the brain—it is also the intimate spiritual and emotional aspects. David says that God knows the secrets of our hearts. The very things that we don't want to admit of ourselves, God knows. Our Creator knows us through and through.

When sin severed the perfect relationship man once held with God, God through Jesus chose to adopt us back into His Kingdom. Adoption was not a part of the Jewish culture like it was the Roman culture. In the Jewish culture, if a male died without an heir, his closest relative would produce an heir with his widow. Paul, a Roman citizen who was familiar with the custom of adoption, could relate what it meant to be adopted into the kingdom of God. It is a new identity with new obligations (old debt and obligations were wiped out), where one becomes an automatic heir—one did not wait until someone died to be heir. The adopted became like the adopter.

> *"For those who are led by the Spirit of God are the children of God. The Spirit you received does not make*

> *you slaves, so that you live in fear again; rather, the Spirit you received brought about your adoption to sonship. And by Him we cry, 'Abba, Father.'*
>
> *The Spirit himself testifies with our spirit that we are God's children. Now if we are children, then we are heirs—heirs of God and co-heirs with Christ, if indeed we share in His sufferings in order that we may also share in His glory."*
>
> Romans 8:14-17

God created us in His image and has a deep great love for us as His image-bearers. We get a glimpse of that love when we are blessed to have children. When a child is in the womb, there is an automatic bond between the child and parent. In the garden, Adam says about Eve,

> *"...this is bone of my bone and flesh of my flesh."*
>
> Genesis 2:23

There is an instant bond and love when one is made from another's image. There is excitement about who the child will take after, the personality traits, looks, and mannerisms they will inherit from their parents. There is unconditional love and delight. Sin did not take away God's love for us; however, it did prevent us from living with Him for eternity. For us to regain our place in heaven, we had to be purchased back.

> *"For He chose us in Him before the creation of the world to be holy and blameless in His sight. In love He predestined us for adoption to sonship through Jesus Christ, in accordance with His pleasure and will— to the praise of His glorious grace, which He has freely given us in the One He loves."*
>
> Ephesians 1:4-6

There are those who have been adopted here on earth who have a great relationship and sense of love and acceptance, and there are those who struggle with the real or perceived rejection or abandonment from their biological parents. There are also those who have experienced a so-called failed adoption, where for whatever reason it did not go the way either party hoped or planned.

The truth is that adoption is a choice. God chose us, fully knowing the decisions we would make and the sins we would commit. To adopt means that one, fully knowing, chooses to take on the debt, problems, hardships, and baggage that comes with the person. God adopted us fully knowing we would still do wrong, cause Him anguish, and mess up.

When I married my husband, I inherited three children. I say inherited, because I chose to be a third parent to them, and I wanted everyone to know they were more to me than just step-children, which unfortunately has been portrayed more times than not as a negative thing or a burden. *Inherit* takes on a different meaning. It is something good being received, a blessing, something of value—a personal treasure.

There were several times that a hardship would come our way and my husband would apologize, saying that this was something I shouldn't have had to deal with or that it was something I didn't sign up for. The truth is, I was aware. I knew when I chose to be a part of my family what I was in for. I may not have known all the situations or the extent of things, but like any relationship or family, I knew we would have bumps and twists and turns from life come our way. I chose my spouse and my family and I made a commitment that no matter what came our way, we were in it together.

Jesus fully knew when He chose to die on the cross what He was dying for—broken, lost, hurting, and depraved people. By choosing to proceed with the Father's plan, He in essence was saying, "They are worth it. I want them as co-heirs to the kingdom of God. I love them and choose them even to death."

Because of Jesus' great love for us, He chose us, even though we were dead in sin, to be restored and redeemed, taking seat with Him in the kingdom of God. Ephesians 2:4-9 says:

> *"But because of His great love for us, God, who is rich in mercy, made us alive with Christ even when we were dead in transgressions—it is by grace you have been saved. And God raised us up with Christ and seated us with Him in the heavenly realms in Christ Jesus, in order that in the coming ages He might show the incomparable riches of His grace, expressed in his kindness to us in Christ Jesus. For it is by grace you have been saved, through faith—and this is not from yourselves, it is the gift of God—not by works, so that no one can boast."*

We did not do anything to deserve the ability to be co-heirs to the kingdom. We cannot work hard enough or do good enough deeds to earn the reward of heaven; nor can we ever in our own efforts obtain it. It was only through God's love and grace that He chose us to be co-heirs and give us the title. Our identity is in Christ Jesus. Our very life and being is from God. The very core of God's nature, His love, is revealed through our sinful nature.

We already know from earlier chapters that we are created in the image of God, possess His attributes, and that we have a purpose. Sin has corrupted and distorted our image and perceptions, which has caused us to many times fall into believing the lies of the enemy; that we are not worthy of love, that we are failures, not valuable, have no purpose, and do not deserve to be treated with respect, care, or importance. The enemy uses these thoughts and internalizations to put a wedge in our relationship with God and others.

Through Jesus' actions on the cross, we can have confidence in who we are because of who He is. In his book, *Living Free in Christ*, Neil T. Anderson listed several verses identifying who we are in Christ and puts them into three categories: our acceptance, our security and our significance.

I have written them below and have also added to it. As you read through them, if any jump out at you, stay on the verse and reflect on it. Ask yourself, which ones have you fully embraced about yourself and our Lord? Which ones do you have a hard time embracing and why?

We are loved and valued

The Lord has chosen you to be His treasured possession (Deuteronomy 14:2). God said this of the Israelites; however, God extended this to all peoples in the New Testament.

> *"I have loved you with an everlasting love; I have drawn you with unfailing kindness."*
>
> Jeremiah 31:3

> *"For God so loved the world that He gave His one and only Son, that whoever believes in Him shall not perish but have eternal life."*
>
> John 3:16

> *"As the Father has loved me, so have I loved you. Now remain in my love."*
>
> John 15:9

> *"I have given them the glory that you gave me, that they may be one as we are one—I in them and you in me—so that they may be brought to complete unity. Then the world will know that you sent me and have loved*

them even as you have loved me."

John 17:22-23

"Therefore, as God's chosen people, holy and dearly loved, clothe yourselves with compassion, kindness, humility, gentleness and patience."

Colossians 3:12

"This is love: not that we loved God, but that He loved us and sent His Son as an atoning sacrifice for our sins."

1 John 4:10

"But you are a chosen people, a royal priesthood, a holy nation, God's special possession, that you may declare the praises of Him who called you out of darkness into His wonderful light."

1 Peter 2:9

"Look at the birds of the air; they do not sow or reap or store away in barns, and yet your heavenly Father feeds them. Are you not much more valuable than they?"

Matthew 6:26

"Consider the ravens: They do not sow or reap, they have no storeroom or barn; yet God feeds them. And how much more valuable you are than birds!"

Luke 12:24

We are wanted and accepted

"Yet to all who did receive Him, to those who believed in His name, He gave the right to become children of God."

John 1:12

"I no longer call you servants, because a servant does not know his master's business. Instead, I have called you friends, for everything that I learned from my Father I have made known to you."

John 15:15

"Therefore, since we have been justified through faith, we have peace with God through our Lord Jesus Christ."

Romans 5:1

"But whoever is united with the Lord is one with Him in spirit."

1 Corinthians 6:17

"You were bought at a price."

1 Corinthians 6:20

"Now you are the body of Christ, and each one of you is a part of it."

1 Corinthians 12:27

"For He chose us in Him before the creation of the world to be holy and blameless in His sight."

Ephesians 1:4

"In love He predestined us for adoption to sonship through Jesus Christ."

Ephesians 1:5

"In Him we were also chosen, having been predestined according to the plan of Him who works out everything in conformity with the purpose of His will."

Ephesians 1:11

"[The Father] has qualified you to share in the inheritance of His holy people in the kingdom of light. For He has rescued us from the dominion of darkness and brought us into the kingdom of the Son He loves, in whom we have redemption, the forgiveness of sins."

Colossians 1:12-14

"For through Him we both have access to the Father by one Spirit."

Ephesians 2:18

"If you belonged to the world, it would love you as its own. As it is, you do not belong to the world, but I have chosen you out of the world."

John 15:19

"For the Son of Man came to seek and to save the lost."

Luke 19:10

We are secure, confident, and free

"There is now no condemnation for those who are in Christ Jesus, because through Christ Jesus the law of the Spirit who gives life has set you free from the law of sin and death."

Romans 8:1-2

"And we know that in all things God works for the good of those who love Him, who have been called according to His purpose."

Romans 8:28

"For you died, and your life is now hidden with Christ in God. When Christ, who is your life, appears, then you

also will appear with Him in glory."

Colossians 3:3-4

"For I am convinced that neither death nor life, neither angels nor demons, neither the present nor the future, nor any powers, neither height nor depth, nor anything else in all creation, will be able to separate us from the love of God that is in Christ Jesus our Lord."

Romans 8:38-39

"Be[ing] confident of this, that he who began a good work in you will carry it on to completion until the day of Christ Jesus."

Philippians 1:6

"I can do all this through Him who gives me strength."

Philippians 4:13

"For the Spirit God gave us does not make us timid, but gives us power, love, and self-discipline."

2 Timothy 1:7

"Let us then approach God's throne of grace with confidence, so that we may receive mercy and find grace to help us in our time of need."

Hebrews 4:16

"The One who was born of God keeps them safe, and the evil one cannot harm them."

1 John 5:18

"In Him and through faith in Him we may approach God with freedom and confidence."

Ephesians 3:12

"But our citizenship is in heaven. And we eagerly await a Savior from there, the Lord Jesus Christ, who, by the power that enables Him to bring everything under His control, will transform our lowly bodies so that they will be like His glorious body."

Philippians 3:20-21

"So we say with confidence, 'The Lord is my helper; I will not be afraid. What can mere mortals do to me?'"

Hebrews 13:6

"This is the confidence we have in approaching God: that if we ask anything according to His will, He hears us."

1 John 5:14

"Now the Lord is the Spirit, and where the Spirit of the Lord is, there is freedom."

2 Corinthians 3:17

"It is for freedom that Christ has set us free. Stand firm, then, and do not let yourselves be burdened again by a yoke of slavery."

Galatians 5:1

"You, my brothers and sisters, were called to be free. But do not use your freedom to indulge the flesh; rather, serve one another humbly in love."

Galatians 5:13

"In Him and through faith in Him we may approach God with freedom and confidence."

Ephesians 3:12

"Blessed and holy are those who share in the first

resurrection. The second death has no power over them, but they will be priests of God and of Christ and will reign with Him for a thousand years."

Revelation 20:6

"Through Him everyone who believes is set free from every sin, a justification you were not able to obtain under the law of Moses."

Acts 13:39

We are significant and full of purpose

"For I know the plans I have for you," declares the Lord, "plans to prosper you and not to harm you, plans to give you hope and a future."

Jeremiah 29:11

"But I have raised you up for this very purpose, that I might show you my power and that my name might be proclaimed in all the earth." (Even though this is talking about Moses, we know God uses us for various purposes and reasons to carry out His will, just as Jesus did.)

Exodus 9:16 (commentary mine)

"You are the salt of the earth."

Matthew 5:13

"You are the light of the world."

Matthew 5:14

"I am the true vine, and my Father is the gardener. He cuts off every branch in me that bears no fruit, while every branch that does bear fruit He prunes so that it

Our value, worth, and purpose

will be even more fruitful."

John 15:1-2

"I am the vine; you are the branches. If you remain in me and I in you, you will bear much fruit; apart from me you can do nothing."

John 15:5

"You did not choose me, but I chose you and appointed you so that you might go and bear fruit—fruit that will last."

John 15:16

"But you will receive power when the Holy Spirit comes on you; and you will be my witnesses in Jerusalem, and in all Judea and Samaria, and to the ends of the earth."

Acts 1:8

"For it is God who works in you to will and to act in order to fulfill His good purpose."

Philippians 2:13

"In a large house there are articles not only of gold and silver, but also of wood and clay; some are for special purposes and some for common use. Those who cleanse themselves from the latter will be instruments for special purposes, made holy, useful to the Master and prepared to do any good work."

2 Timothy 2:20-21

"What, after all, is Apollos? And what is Paul? Only servants, through whom you came to believe—as the Lord has assigned to each his task. I planted the seed,

Apollos watered it, but God has been making it grow. So neither the one who plants nor the one who waters is anything, but only God, who makes things grow. The one who plants and the one who waters have one purpose, and they will each be rewarded according to their own labor. For we are co-workers in God's service; you are God's field, God's building."

1 Corinthians 3:5-9

"Don't you know that you yourselves are God's temple and that God's Spirit dwells in your midst? If anyone destroys God's temple, God will destroy that person; for God's temple is sacred, and you together are that temple."

1 Corinthians 3:16-17

"Therefore, if anyone is in Christ, the new creation has come: The old has gone, the new is here! All this is from God, who reconciled us to Himself through Christ and gave us the ministry of reconciliation: that God was reconciling the world to Himself in Christ, not counting people's sins against them. And He has committed to us the message of reconciliation. We are therefore Christ's ambassadors, as though God were making His appeal through us.

We implore you on Christ's behalf: Be reconciled to God."

2 Corinthians 5:17-20

"And God raised us up with Christ and seated us with Him in the heavenly realms in Christ Jesus."

Ephesians 2:6

"For we are God's handiwork, created in Christ Jesus

Our Value, Worth, and Purpose

to do good works, which God prepared in advance for us to do."

Ephesians 2:10

The Foundation of Our Identity

The enemy uses our insecurities, negative self perceptions, and the hurtful comments or behaviors of others to shake our identity. The only way to combat the negative inner tape is with the truth of who God is and who He says we are. If our foundation is not sturdy and secured on that truth, or if we are unwilling to believe and accept what God says about who we are, we will continue to hurt and give the enemy a foothold over us.

Even when it is hard to believe these truths because of wounds or scars, we must rely on faith and trust in God's unchanging and unfailing character. If you want to learn more about God's faithful love towards us even when we turn from Him, read through the Old Testament book of Judges. Time and time again the Israelites turn from God, yet God continuously shows the Israelites that He loves them and has good things planned for them. God is constant and faithful in character!

Jesus Is the Cornerstone of Our Faith

Think about what it takes to build a structure. First the foundation must be secure. Once the foundation is firm and solid, you can develop the base of the structure (cornerstone) and start building up. Once the structure is built, the building must be utilized to fulfill its purpose. A building not used may be great to look at and still maintain worth—however, it serves no purpose.

God created you just the way He wants you! He has great things planned for you, and no matter what wrongs you do, He will never deny or take back your value and worth.

We need to keep placing our value and worth where it belongs and to whom it belongs—our Heavenly Father.

LIVING OUT YOUR FAITH

Gary Sibcy says,

> *"Spirituality is about how well our thinking, feeling, behaving, relating, communicating, and problem-solving operate in relation to God and others."*

Spiritual growth

Spiritual growth occurs when we take what we know about God and align ourselves with it amid any and all circumstances. Even when we have a hard time believing, it is acting out of obedience what we know based on what God has told us.

Bernard of Clairvaux founded 70 monasteries and was the leader of the monastery at Clairvaux, France. He was a great lover of God and considered the last of the Church Fathers. In his writing, *The Love of God,* he explains that divine love is how we grow and develop in God's perfect love found in Jesus Christ. He presents Four Degrees of Love, which are a model for spiritual development in Christlikeness.

The first is: *I love me for my sake* (selfish love).

I love me for myself and expect you to build me up in how I love myself. One must come to realize that God loves us and He is the source of how we can love others.

The second is: *I love God for my sake* (dependence on God).

People who are animal and carnal by instinct, who only know what it means to love themselves, can begin to love God for their own blessing. This love is still about *me,* in that it's about what God can do for me, but it's a start to at least going to God, even if for own benefit.

The third is: *I love God for God's own sake* (intimacy with God).

God loving us is a miracle of grace. It's in God's character to love: He created us and died for us. I love God because of what He did for me.

The fourth is: *I love me for God's sake* (being united with God's love).

I can display my life for God's glory.

To achieve this fourth degree of love we must love ourselves. This is very difficult for some people. To love ourselves in this way is to not just know what God says about who we—who *you*—are; it also means you believe and accept His love for you and that you have peace in your true identity. It's changing the question from "Am I lovable?" or "Do you love me?" to a confident statement that "I am lovable."

As one grows in spiritual maturity, she gains a deeper understanding of God's love. Her life and will starts to conform to that of God's will and desire for her life. We cannot judge where another is on their spiritual journey; but we should encourage others to continue to grow in their understanding of who God is and what it means to not just believe, but surrender their life to Him.

God is the one who pursues a relationship with us. He created us, loves us and desires us to respond in obedience to Him. It is through the Spirit's softening of our hearts that we respond to His call and that we grow spiritually. If left up to us, we would continue down a path of destruction and moral corruptness. If left to us, we would never pursue God. It is only because God the Father pursues us, because Jesus died for us, and because we have the Spirit to reveal the void in our lives, that we can hear, see, experience, and respond to God's pursuit.

We do not know who will respond to God; but it is still our responsibility to share the gospel with everyone in our sphere of influence. Many sermons have been preached on the parable of the growing seed. Mark 4:2-20 says:

> *"He taught them many things by parables, and in His teaching, said: 'Listen! A farmer went out to sow his seed. As he was scattering the seed, some fell along the path, and the birds came and ate it up. Some fell on rocky places, where it did not have much soil. It sprang up quickly, because the soil was shallow. But when the sun came up, the plants were scorched, and they withered because they had no root. Other seed fell among thorns, which grew up and choked the plants, so that they did not bear grain. Still other seed fell on good soil. It came up, grew and produced a crop, some multiplying thirty, some sixty, some a hundred times.'*

Then Jesus said,

> *'Whoever has ears to hear, let them hear.'*
> *When He was alone, the Twelve and the others around Him asked Him about the parables. He told them, 'The secret of the kingdom of God has been given to you. But to those on the outside everything is said in parables so that*
> *"they may be ever seeing but never perceiving,*
> *'and ever hearing but never understanding;*
> *'otherwise they might turn and be forgiven!"*

> *Then Jesus said to them, 'Don't you understand this parable? How then will you understand any parable? The farmer sows the word.*
>
> *Some people are like seed along the path, where the word is sown. As soon as they hear it, Satan comes and takes away the word that was sown in them.*
>
> *Others, like seed sown on rocky places, hear the word and at once receive it with joy. But since they have no root, they last only a short time. When trouble or persecution comes because of the word, they quickly fall away.*
>
> *Still others, like seed sown among thorns, hear the word; but the worries of this life, the deceitfulness of wealth and the desires for other things come in and choke the word, making it unfruitful.*
>
> *Others, like seed sown on good soil, hear the word, accept it, and produce a crop—some thirty, some sixty, some a hundred times what was sown.'"*

There will be people who outright reject God. There will be some who hear the truth of the gospel, but because they have no fixed principle, will come and go when they need or desire. There will be those who receive it with gladness, but then don't act on it or surrender their lives to God.

We need to be the seed that was rooted in the good soil. We must grow our roots deep so we do not get uprooted or shaken by false teachings or differing doctrines. We need to grow our roots deep, so when trials come we can endure and not wither away. We need to grow our roots deep so that we can flourish and produce fruit—healthy fruit from the Spirit that enables us to live godly lives and be a testimony to others of God's goodness.

These are the fruits of love, joy, peace, patience, kindness, goodness, faithfulness, gentleness, and self-control. Outside of the Spirit, these fruits cannot be produced, because once conflict comes, our self-preservation and defenses or negative reactivity come up. It is during hard circumstances or when facing persecution that these fruits bear great testimony of God's greatness to others. It is also in these times where we ourselves experience spiritual growth.

We also need to seek spiritual growth by getting involved in the church. I don't just mean the *local* church, or even necessarily the church *building*. We must surround ourselves with other believers who will encourage us, mentor us, and challenge us.

We need a support system who is there when life becomes challenging or when we start to question or doubt. We need to be plugged into a ministry where we are using our gifts, talents, and abilities to serve others, building the kingdom, and being alive in how God made us.

We need to have a place where we are also receiving and hearing truth, so we can grow in our understanding of scripture. If we are not growing, then we are not being effective in bringing glory to God. If we are not conversing and challenging each other in the word, then we are susceptible to misinterpretations, false teaching and leading, and stunted growth.

As Paul says in Ephesians 4:14-16,

> *"Then we will no longer be infants, tossed back and forth by the waves, and blown here and there by every wind of teaching and by the cunning and craftiness of people in their deceitful scheming. Instead, speaking the truth in love, we will grow to become in every respect the mature body of him who is the head, that is, Christ. From him the whole body, joined and held together by every supporting ligament, grows and builds itself up in love, as each part does its work."*

Perseverance

The Christian life is not easy: in fact, it is guaranteed to have challenges. Scripture is full of suffering, obstacles, and hardships; yet as we see time and time again, God's character shines through as people graciously (and some not so graciously) persevere through.

It is how we respond to these challenges that will cause us to grow spiritually. It is by enduring distress and suffering in the present while believing and hoping in a future outcome through faith of who God is that we are shown what God can do. Even if the outcome isn't what we had hoped, it is still maintaining the confidence of God's power, goodness, and glory.

> *"Consider it pure joy, my brothers and sisters, whenever you face trials of many kinds, because you know that the testing of your faith produces perseverance. Let perseverance finish its work so that you may be mature and complete, not lacking anything."*
>
> James 1:2-4

> *"Then they returned to Lystra, Iconium and Antioch, strengthening the disciples and encouraging them to remain true to the faith. 'We must go through many hardships to enter the kingdom of God,' they said."*
>
> Acts 14:21-22

> *"In the presence of God and of Christ Jesus, who will judge the living and the dead, and in view of His appearing and His kingdom, I give you this charge: Preach the word; be prepared in season and out of season; correct, rebuke and encourage—with great patience and careful*

> *instruction. For the time will come when people will not put up with sound doctrine. Instead, to suit their own desires, they will gather around them a great number of teachers to say what their itching ears want to hear. They will turn their ears away from the truth and turn aside to myths. But you, keep your head in all situations, endure hardship, do the work of an evangelist, discharge all the duties of your ministry."*
>
> 2 Timothy 4:1-5

> *"In all this you greatly rejoice, though now for a little while you may have had to suffer grief in all kinds of trials. These have come so that the proven genuineness of your faith—of greater worth than gold, which perishes even though refined by fire—may result in praise, glory and honor when Jesus Christ is revealed."*
>
> 1 Peter 1:6-7

We live in a broken world, and because of that we will experience pain, hurt, destruction, and anguish. Since the dawn of original sin, we have an enemy whose goal is to keep us from a relationship with God and the life God desires for us.

From our inherited sin, we bring upon ourselves hardships and trouble. Not only that, but the sins of others affect us directly and indirectly. It is out of sin and brokenness of this world apart from God that we have death, disease, moral corruption, addiction, mental disorder, selfishness, lust, pride, and the list goes on. It is in a hardship, or *thorn in the flesh* as Paul calls it, that God replies,

> *"My grace is sufficient for you."*
>
> 2 Corinthians 12:9

Hardships should not come as a surprise, but rather a guarantee of what we will endure because of our faith and because of the world's brokenness and separation from God. Not only are we expected to endure hardships, but because we have an adversary, an enemy of God, we are to also expect temptations.

Satan and his legion of fallen angels are crafty and their goal is to keep us from not only having a relationship with God, but also to put a wedge in our relationship with others. In the Garden of Eden, Satan tempted Eve with the fruit of the knowledge of good and evil. He created confusion of God's commands (*"If you touch it you would surely die."*), caused Eve to question God's goodness, to presume upon God's power, and to rob God of honor by giving in to Satan through disobedience. Satan's aim in temptation is to bring us to sin against God.

He tempted Jesus similarly to how he did with Eve in the garden and how he continues to tempt others, including us today.

> *"Then Jesus was led by the Spirit into the wilderness to be tempted by the devil. After fasting forty days and forty nights, He was hungry. The tempter came to Him and said, 'If you are the Son of God, tell these stones to become bread.'*
> *Jesus answered, 'It is written: 'Man shall not live on bread alone, but on every word that comes from the mouth of God.'"*
> *Then the devil took Him to the holy city and had Him stand on the highest point of the temple. 'If you are the Son of God,' he said, 'throw yourself down. For it is written "He will command his angels concerning you, and they will lift you up in their hands, so that you will not strike your foot against a stone."*
> *Jesus answered him, 'It is also written: 'Do not put the Lord your God to the test.'"*
> *Again, the devil took Him to a very high mountain*

> *and showed Him all the kingdoms of the world and their splendor. 'All this I will give you,' he said, 'if you will bow down and worship me.'*
>
> *Jesus said to him, 'Away from me, Satan! For it is written: 'Worship the Lord your God, and serve Him only."*
>
> *Then the devil left Him, and angels came and attended Him."*
>
> Matthew 4:1-11

First, Satan tempted Jesus with food, knowing He was weak and hungry after a 40-day fast. Note how Satan wasn't just offering Jesus food; he was telling Jesus to take control of his own need and provision by doing it Himself. Think about areas in your life where you are weighed down, tired, and ready to be over a particular situation. Sometimes it feels like it would just be easier, more convenient, to cave in this one time, or take control because of impatience with God's timing or doubting God's word and goodness for us. Satan isn't stupid. He knows to prey on the areas where we are weak, where there is tension, or when we are tired of waiting; and that is where he strikes.

Second, Satan tempted Jesus through challenging God's protection and abusing scripture. Just because God saved Daniel from the lion's den, does not mean we are to walk up to wild lions and expect God to protect us. It is arrogant to act like or think that God is at our beck and call.

God is not at our command, nor is He our personal genie to perform magic tricks to impress others. God does not have to prove Himself to us or to others.

Satan used, or rather abused, scripture to tempt and try to hurt Jesus by encouraging Jesus to throw Himself off the temple to His death. Jesus used scripture to put Satan back in his place and combat the temptation. Just to be clear, Jesus was not tempted to throw Himself off the building, but the set-up was for Jesus to prove Himself as God, or for God the Father to prove His faithfulness. It was a trick of the enemy to try to get Jesus to do something that was unnecessary and to take focus off God.

Similarly, Satan also misuses scripture with us to prevent us from experiencing God's peace and truth. Let's go back to the example of the lions; some may say if a lion attacked you, then you didn't have enough faith in God or He would have protected you. What horrible abuse of God's word! This plays into the hands of the enemy by twisting or misapplying scripture.

We have a responsibility to understand scripture, so when the enemy or others are abusing it, we can state truth and squelch the lies that cause damage. Whether God chooses to do something or not is up to God: our job is to maintain our faith and obedience. Taking scripture out of context and misusing it or abusing it for personal agenda or as a feel-good prosperity belief is dangerous, too.

Third, we see that Satan tempted Jesus with power. How funny is it that Jesus, being God and co-creator of everything, is being tempted with something He already has? But there is more to it. Satan changed his strategy. Satan started out trying to get Jesus to question God's goodness in provision and security, hitting on the physical, emotional, and mental aspects of man's needs. Now, Satan has shifted to the grand allure of desire and want. Notice how he took Jesus up to a high mountaintop where the scenery was beautiful, breathtaking, and eye-catching. Satan is trying to convince Jesus that He does not have to follow the will of the Father, that He can have glory and splendor now.

As we see by Jesus' response, Satan has crossed the line. Jesus has had enough of his shenanigans and commands him to leave. Jesus saw through the deceit of the enemy and knew that Satan was trying to get

Him to reject His Father, and to give worship and glory that belongs to the Father to Satan.

Through these temptations, Satan's messages were along the lines of, "If God cared, you wouldn't be suffering. God has abandoned you. You don't need to wait for God; you can do it yourself, have it all for yourself now. God doesn't want the best for you, you need to look after your own interests. If God loved you, He would have provided for you, protected you."

Notice that Jesus quoted scripture, and not just any scripture, but Deuteronomy 6 and 8 in which God tells us to keep His commands in our heart. If we do not keep God's words in our heart, then we will easily be sifted like wheat (Luke 22:31). Deuteronomy 8 also tells how God tested the Israelites' hearts and obedience to His commands. It is important to note that God *tests* His people and their obedience to Him; however, God never *tempts* us into sinning. To sin is one hundred percent on us.

God says in scripture that He will provide us the strength needed to endure temptation (1 Corinthians 10:13). God will provide a way out, either by removing the trial, or equipping us to endure the trial. God does not set us up for failure, but provides us with opportunity to grow and experience more of Him.

It is neat to notice throughout scripture that with testing, God also blesses. When we persevere through temptations, God is honored.

God allows Satan to test us, as we will later see in Job—the original word used here for test is equated with tempting, to entice one to sin. God also tests us as seen with the Israelites—this being different in that the word means to show something is acceptable and good.

Testing is an opportunity for us to persevere in obedience and bring glory to God. We should never expect blessings in return for perseverance, but God grows us through the endurance, and that in and of itself is a spiritual blessing.

Righteous living

Ephesians 5:15-17 says,

> *"Be very careful, then, how you live—not as unwise but as wise, making the most of every opportunity, because the days are evil. Therefore, do not be foolish, but understand what the Lord's will is."*

There is subtlety in Satan's temptations. There is a play on desires and there also seems to be a false sense of innocence. The first two ways in which Satan tempted needed wisdom to discern; the last was a strong temptation, which needed resolution to resist; yet Satan was put in his place in each situation. Jesus recalled God's word and used God's word to defeat the temptations of the enemy.

Just as Jesus used God's word to combat the lies and deceit of the enemy, we too must go to scripture. The best reference for how to approach the hardships of life and the cunning temptations of the enemy is found in Ephesians 6:10-18.

> *"Finally, be strong in the Lord and in his mighty power. Put on the full armor of God, so that you can take your stand against the devil's schemes. For our struggle is not against flesh and blood, but against the rulers, against the authorities, against the powers of this dark world and against the spiritual forces of evil in the heavenly realms.*
> *Therefore put on the full armor of God, so that when the day of evil comes, you may be able to stand your ground, and after you have done everything, to stand.*

> *Stand firm then, with the belt of truth buckled around your waist, with the breastplate of righteousness in place, and with your feet fitted with the readiness that comes from the gospel of peace.*
>
> *In addition to all this, take up the shield of faith, with which you can extinguish all the flaming arrows of the evil one. Take the helmet of salvation and the sword of the Spirit, which is the word of God. And pray in the Spirit on all occasions with all kinds of prayers and requests. With this in mind, be alert and always keep on praying for all the Lord's people."*

The first thing to notice is, it is the Lord's power and strength that we are to rely on. We are powerless without God.

Second, note that putting on the armor is an action step which we choose to do… or *not* to do. If we choose not to, then we cannot be surprised when we are overtaken by sin and destructiveness, nor can we have any other person or thing to blame except ourselves. We are not called to put on the armor when we are in the midst of a battle, or when we finally recognize the battle in before us.

The battle began long before we existed. The war has already been won; however, we have an adversary who knows his time is limited and wants to create as much turmoil and dissention as possible for God's people.

Our armor must be on whether we are actively engaged in the battle or whether we are in the reserves, because we will never know when the enemy will strike.

Our armor starts with the belt of truth. This truth is the word of God found in scripture. It is the gospel of salvation which leads us to righteous living. It is what keeps us centered and allows us to go about freely without getting caught up in legalistic views or false teachings. The truth is, we have a savior who made us acceptable to God and there are no additions to, or extra requirements for, salvation.

The second piece of armor is the breastplate of righteousness, which is our spiritual life and growth in the Lord. 2 Corinthians 4:16 says that we are being renewed day by day. This is part of the sanctification process in which we are being made more like Christ and bearing the fruits of His image. We must be in God's word and seek His truth in order to grow.

The breastplate functions as a protective barrier for the heart and vital organs. We are told in Proverbs 4:23 to guard our heart for it is the wellspring of life. This means we need to guard ourselves from gossip, slander, perverse talk, lust, coveting, manipulation, jealousy, and all things that stunt our spiritual growth and prevent us from bearing fruit and having the pleasing aroma of Christ that attracts others into a relationship with God.

One of my favorite verses is Proverbs 27:19 which says,

> *"As water reflects a face, so a man's heart reflects the man."*

Our character is our defense. 1 Thessalonians 5:8 tells us to put on the breastplate of faith and love. This is faith in Jesus Christ and love towards others, as modeled by Him. The same grace in which we were given, we are to extend to one another.

The third part of the armor mentioned is regarding our feet. Having our feet fitted with the readiness of the gospel of peace means that we are ready to advance when we need to advance, and ready to hold ground when we need to hold ground. Just as the gospel of truth centers us, the gospel of peace keeps us grounded. This peace is of the Spirit in which we have confidence and security of who God is, and what He can do, no matter the situation or circumstance.

Having a unity of peace with other believers enables us to maintain a united front and makes us stronger. As Ecclesiastes 4:12 says,

> *"Though one may be overpowered,*
> *two can defend themselves.*
> *A cord of three strands is not quickly broken."*

We need to be among a community of believers. We need to have sisters and brothers in Christ who will stand beside us, and us beside them, in unity. This will result in an even stronger foundation than we can maintain individually. Paul says in Ephesians 4:3 that it is our responsibility to make every effort to keep the unity of peace. We keep this peace by being gentle, patient, and loving towards each other. We are to extend the same grace and forgiveness that Christ did when He died on the cross for us. Pride gets in the way of unity and leads to downfall.

Paul requires us to act when he commands us to *take* the next three parts of the armor.

First, we are to *take up* the shield of faith. This means that we have confidence in what God can do. We do not sit and worry over a situation, but trust in God's goodness, no matter how He chooses to respond. It is an attitude of humility and dependency on God in the most adverse situations. It is committed obedience, no matter what, while trusting and believing in God's goodness to see you through.

Darts of the enemy are designed to wound the soul. They come swiftly and when you least suspect them. This makes me think of poisonous darts that indigenous people used to paralyze or kill their target. They would get their poison from poisonous serpents or plants. Visually the dart doesn't seem to do much visual damage; however, the unseen poison is where the danger lies.

When Paul wrote this passage about putting on the armor of God, spears and arrows were actually destructive beyond their appearance. The fiery darts Paul referred to were originally arrows wrapped with cloth and doused with flammable liquid which was lit and fired upon the enemy. These arrows did not always maintain the flame, so weapon designers adapted the arrows to contain flammable liquid that instantly created a fiery combustion upon hitting the target.

Roman soldiers would douse their armor in water so if they were struck with a flaming arrow, they would be protected. The shield is to protect us from these fiery darts that are meant to paralyze, incapacitate, and wound us. We must douse our shield in the truth of who God is. Faith is not just *knowing* God's goodness, but *believing* God's goodness, and when we act upon that belief, the fiery darts are quenched and rendered ineffective.

When distracted, we may we let our guard down and get hit by a dart from the enemy. When that happens, we are to pick up the shield and combat the shame, fear, negative inner tape, or whatever the enemy is using to prevent us from experiencing the fullness of God. We will talk more about how to do this when we talk about the last piece of armor.

Second, we are to take the helmet of salvation. The most vulnerable part of a soldier during battle is his head. Like the breastplate, the helmet protects a vital part of the body—the head, brain, mind. Since we surrendered our lives to Christ, we are being sanctified, renewed inwardly day by day, and molded more and more into His image (Colossians 3).

Isaiah 59:16-17 says,

> *"His own arm worked out salvation for him and his own righteousness sustained him. He put on righteousness as his breastplate and the helmet of salvation on his head."*

Salvation is more than just being saved from hell; it is having a life and eternal future with God. We have hope because of what Jesus accomplished on the cross. It is when we lose sight of the hope we have that we get discouraged, depressed, and troubled in mind and spirit.

Paul compares our armor to that of God's when battling Satan. Just as Satan tempted Jesus to prove His godliness and to dishonor God, Satan tempts us to despair and question God's goodness for us, as well as challenges our faith in God. We do not need to prove anything to Satan. Our battlefield of the mind is where we must stop internalizing the external influences that contribute to the negative tape of worthlessness and where we must claim God's truths of value, worth, acceptance, and love.

Throughout history, the design of a helmet would change as new weapons were made, in order to provide the most adequate protection. We know that Satan doesn't stick with one strategy for temptation, and so we too must broaden our protection by growing in God's words and spiritual maturity. We must claim hope; hope of what is to come, and hope of what God is currently doing, because of our salvation in Christ.

Each army's helmet is unique in representing its ruling kingdom, and it can also help to identify friend from foe. Our helmet represents our good and faithful God. Our helmet symbolizes our already victorious Lord over the enemy. We go into battle with confidence because we are wearing a helmet of salvation, a helmet of hope, and a helmet of security.

> *"But since we belong to the day, let us be self-controlled, putting on faith and love as a breastplate, and the hope of salvation as the helmet. For God did not appoint us to suffer a wrath but to receive salvation through our Lord Jesus Christ. He died for us so that, whether we are awake or asleep, we may live together with Him."*
>
> 1 Thessalonians 5:8-10 (CSB)

The final piece of armor is the sword of the Spirit. The sword takes more of an offensive than defensive approach in that it is attacking or engaging the enemy head on. There is a saying that "the best defense is a good offense." Basically, a strong offensive action, rather than a passive one, which for us is the word of God, will hinder our enemy and his opposition or counterattack towards us.

We do not overcome the enemy by our own will, power, knowledge, or anything else except the word of God. This is the word of God through scripture and we must constantly go to it. Just as Jesus used the word when encountering the enemy, we too must be in the word in order to combat the enemy. This requires taking every thought captive, affirming our identity, revealing God's plan, and directing our lives in obedience to the Lord's will.

Outside of putting on the armor of God, we are told to pray on all occasions with all kinds of prayers and requests, including praises. We are to pray continually, without ceasing. Why? Prayer connects us to God, His heart, His will, and helps us tap into the Spirit of God to access His character traits that we need in our lives, such as peace, mercy, grace, love, and forgiveness.

Prayer softens our own heart attitude to situations and people. Even when we don't know how to pray, or know the words to use, we are told that the Spirit helps us and intercedes for us through groans that words cannot express (Romans 8:26). We are not just called to pray for ourselves, but for others as well.

> *"I urge, then, first of all, that requests, prayers, intercession and thanksgiving be made for all people—for kings and all those in authority, that we may live peaceful and quiet lives in all godliness and holiness. This is good, and pleases God our Savior, who wants all people to be saved and to come to a knowledge of the truth."*
>
> 1 Timothy 2:1-4

> *"Is anyone among you in trouble? Let them pray. Is anyone happy? Let them sing songs of praise. Is anyone among you sick? Let them call the elders of the church to pray over them and anoint them with oil in the name of the Lord.*
> *And the prayer offered in faith will make the sick person well; the Lord will raise them up. If they have sinned, they will be forgiven. Therefore confess your sins to each other and pray for each other so that you may be healed. The prayer of a righteous person is powerful and effective."*
>
> James 5:13-16

Praising God reminds us of His faithfulness, goodness, and of all the ways He has and does bless us, protect us, and give us all we need to persevere and endure. Praise takes the focus off the situation that seems so big, and puts the focus on God and His power. Praise also keeps us from falling into the trap of focusing on the enemy and what the enemy is doing, rather than focusing on God and glorifying God for what He has done and can do.

Remember, the enemy wants our focus off worshiping God. We must make a conscious effort to keep our worship on God, and to continuously redirect it back to God. Worship is key, because that is the very thing that Satan envies and desires for himself.

We can be in many spiritual conversations or debates which seem to be heavenly focused; but sometimes it is not. We can get caught up in the content of things and totally miss the bigger picture.

> *"Be joyful always, pray continually, give thanks in all circumstances; for this is God's will for you in Christ Jesus.*
> *Do not put out the Spirit's fire. Do not treat prophecies with contempt. Test everything. Hold on to what is good. Avoid every kind of evil.*
> *May God Himself, the God of peace, sanctify you through and through. May your whole spirit, soul and body be kept blameless at the coming of our Lord Jesus Christ. The One who calls you is faithful, and He will do it."*
> 1 Thessalonians 5:16-24

> *"Be patient, then, brothers and sisters, until the Lord's coming. See how the farmer waits for the land to yield its valuable crop, patiently waiting for the autumn and spring rains. You too, be patient and stand firm, because the Lord's coming is near. Don't grumble against one another, brothers, or you will be judged. The Judge is standing at the door!*
> *Brothers and sisters, as an example of patience in the face of suffering, take the prophets who spoke in the name of the Lord. As you know, we consider blessed those who have persevered. You have heard of Job's perseverance and have seen what the Lord finally brought about. The Lord is full of compassion and mercy."*
> James 5:7-11

It is through the hard times that we grow deeper and learn even more about God. It is easy to forget our dependency when we are no longer white-knuckled and clinging to God for every moment. It is in the waiting, in the persevering, and in the sustaining that we grow more spiritually and praise more continually.

Trusting God's goodness

It is guaranteed that we will experience trials, struggles, and temptations, but we have all we need to stand firm during them. Job is a great example for us. It is important for us to recognize that nothing happens without the Lord's approval, and even with approval, God sets boundaries on what the enemy can do.

In the case of Job, God said his life was not to be touched. The reason for the testing, or what seemed like punishment for Job, really wasn't about Job as much as it was about God's glory and the accuser being proven wrong. The severity of Job's testing increased all the more as Job remained standing strong in God's goodness.

In Job's first test, he faced: loss of all his cattle through a raid, loss of his sheep through a fire by lightning, loss of his camels through another raid, death to most of his servants, and then, as he was still processing these events, a tornado that swept through and killed his sons, daughters, and oldest brother. All this occurred one after another, within moments, as he was feasting with his family.

Job's response? In great loss and brokenness, Job tore his clothes, shaved his head, and fell to the ground in worship. Yes, you read it right—in worship! Job's faith in the goodness of God allowed him to praise God even amid such devastation.

God was greatly pleased with Job, but Satan could not stand to be proven wrong and for God to be worshiped through it, so he thought he could get Job to curse God by attacking Job's body. He declared,

> *"A man will give all he has for his own life."*
>
> Job 2:4

God allowed Satan to inflict physical suffering on Job, but said his life was to be spared. Satan did not hold back. Job was afflicted with painful festering sores all over his body, scabs that peeled and became black, nightmares, disfigurement and revolting appearance, bad breath, fever, extreme weight loss, and pain day and night. Can you imagine? I would not wish this on anyone. The pain and sores were so bad that Job took broken pottery pieces and scraped himself to find some sort of relief.

Amazingly, through all of this, Job did not sin in the things he did and said. He maintained his integrity and faith in the goodness of God.

As if the physical and mental torment wasn't enough, Job's own wife encourages him to curse God and get the suffering over with.

> *"His wife said to him, 'Are you still holding on to your integrity? Curse God and die!' He replied, 'You are talking like a foolish woman. Shall we accept good from God and not trouble?'"*
>
> Job 2:9-10

Job held onto his faith in God's character. Job knew that no matter what the circumstance, God is constant in His character. At first his friends sit with him to grieve the suffering, but because they can't make sense of this trial, and didn't know God's higher purpose for it, they took some truths about God out of context.

It is interesting that at first, they sat quietly with Job, which is a soothing act for someone who is grieving. Perhaps the silence made them uncomfortable after a certain period of time and they thought they needed to do or say something. Perhaps they couldn't make sense of the circumstances themselves and it created unwanted feelings. In arrogance, they presumed upon things in which they did not know, claiming knowledge they did not have.

They make the false assumption that Job must have sinned against God to deserve this much punishment, that Job needed to repent and humble himself. He is accused of being a hypocrite. He is accused of mocking God. His friends judge and condemn him, make cruel insinuations about him, and reprimand him.

Throughout the lengthy dialogues and accusations, Job claims innocence; but his body, mind, and spirit are in despair. Job asks God to reassure him that he has not done anything wrong like his friends are saying. When God does not respond, Job starts to question God's goodness. Why is God punishing him?

Not much has changed for us today when we experience a prolonged season of suffering. We too can get to a place of uncertainty and even doubt. In Ecclesiastes, we are told that we become like mad men when we are oppressed repeatedly without respite. No wonder Job starts to question.

In Job's brokenness and weak spirit, Job thinks that God is getting pleasure out of oppressing an innocent man. He even accused God of delighting in the wicked. Because of Job's suffering, he is not in the right state of mind to argue theology. As Job continues to defend his innocence to his friends and wrestles all night trying to understand God, and demanding an explanation from God, he eventually comes to the acceptance that though God has given man wisdom, we are limited in our wisdom.

Upon this, God finally speaks and it silences the enemy, the friends, and Job (Job 38-42). God did not answer Job's questions, but rather questioned Job himself by powerfully stating things like,

> "Where were you when I laid the earth's foundation?"
>
> Job 38:4

> "Have you comprehended the vast expanses of the earth?"
>
> Job 38:18

> "Do you have an arm like God's and can your voice thunder like His?"
>
> Job 40:9

Isaiah 29:16 says,

> "You turn things upside down, as if the potter were thought to be like the clay! Shall what is formed say to the one who formed it, "You did not make me"? Can the pot say to the potter, "You know nothing?"

Even though Job maintained his obedience, there is regret because of his hasty words in time of suffering. Where it would be understandable that someone would want vindication for the accusations his friends put on him, Job prays for them. It is important to note that the offense of the friends was not against Job, but more against God. While Job made mistakes in his attitude and thinking, the friends spoke more theological truths; however, they had more spiritual arrogance than spiritual knowledge or understanding of these truths they spoke.

God answered Job's prayer in having mercy on them, and God blessed Job for his virtue and gave him twice what he had before the testing. Job's question of "Why?" was never answered. The *why* is irrelevant, as the answer is more about having faith in God's goodness, even when things go far beyond the power of human wisdom and understanding.

The prophet Habakkuk asked a similar question. God told him to "live by faith." God does not have to give us a reason, nor can He be held to account for His actions. We are to trust and live by faith. We are to take the focus off what we don't know, and put it on what we do know, which is how we are to live no matter what the circumstance.

For Job, the hardship was not because of anything he did, but rather what Satan was doing to him. But this is not always the case. Many times we blame Satan, when really it is our own self who plays a major role in our hardship.

Take the parable of the prodigal son, for example. This younger son was not happy with where he was, so he asked his father for his portion of the inheritance, took all his possessions and went to a new country to live life the way he wanted. The son chose to live a wild life and spent all his money doing as he pleased—for a season.

Broke and without a home, he ended up working by feeding pigs, which was an unclean animal for the Jews and would be considered a degrading and detestable job. He was so poor and hungry that he even desired to eat the pigs' leftovers. At this, scripture says he came to his senses and in humility recognized his sin. He would go back to his father and throw himself down at his mercy, hopefully be considered not as a son, but as a man for hire.

> *"So he got up and went to his father. But while he was still a long way off, his father saw him and was filled with compassion for him; he ran to his son, threw his arms around him and kissed him.*
>
> *The son said to him, 'Father, I have sinned against heaven and against you. I am no longer worthy to be called your son.'*
>
> *But the father said to his servants, 'Quick! Bring the best robe and put it on him. Put a ring on his finger and sandals on his feet. Bring the fattened calf and kill*

> *it. Let's have a feast and celebrate. For this son of mine was dead and is alive again; he was lost and is found.' So they began to celebrate."*
>
> Luke 15:20-24

The father didn't give an, "I told you so." No, the father ran to his son, had compassion on him, and put a robe, ring, and sandals on him, which symbolized position and acceptance. The father even had the fattened calf killed, which is reserved for special occasions and the choice meat of the herd which makes it very valuable.

After we see the father's response, we get an opposite and very contrasting response from the older brother. He was bitter and resentful because he was the one who maintained his position, took care of his responsibilities, and didn't ask the father for anything, not even a cheap celebration with friends. Now back comes his younger brother, who did much wrong, and he is given such elaborate treatment? It doesn't seem fair, does it?

Many times, as Christians, we adopt the behavior of the older brother. We feel that we deserve to be blessed, recognized, or given special treatment because we have obeyed and maintained righteous living. And if it isn't enough to expect to be rewarded, we compare lifestyle choices and think it unjust that someone who is not making godly choices is given something beyond what we ourselves have received.

As Christians, we should be joyous for a person who is receiving gifts, instead of having a heart attitude of jealousy and resentment. The interesting thing here is that the father says,

> *"You are always with me, and everything I have is yours."*
>
> Luke 15: 31

Basically, the father is saying, "blessings are at your disposal and you have access to all I have." This is confirmed in Ephesians 1:3: that we are given every spiritual blessing. The truth is that the further one has fallen in their depravity, the more one understands and is aware of the grace of God. Blessed are those who have not had to fall as hard or far before surrendering their lives to God.

When we start comparing our lives, our testimonial experiences, or our blessings, we take the focus off the glory of what God has done in our life, and rather than rejoicing together in the grace and mercy of God, we camp outside of the celebration and stew on bitterness and self-centeredness which robs us of joy.

If this has been you, it is time to confess, repent of the attitude, and join back in the celebration with others who have missed seeing you there.

There is one more illustration or example to bring up before we move on to our final chapter. This is the description we have seen in most children's Bible stories, which is the lamb being carried on the shoulders of the shepherd. Perhaps you have not stopped to wonder why the lamb is being carried. Maybe you have come up with some cutesy reasons why, mostly because the lamb itself is just a fun, innocent-looking ball of fluff. The truth is, the shepherd intentionally broke the lamb's leg. Harsh? Well, let's put it in context.

The shepherd's job is to protect and care for the sheep, no matter the cost. There are wolves and other predators nearby, and the shepherd does not want to lose even one of his sheep. As we can all laugh and relate, there is always that *one* who is a little more stubborn than the others, always challenging the boundaries. Sheep are no different.

If the shepherd notices a lamb is missing, he will leave the herd and go search for that lost lamb. That one lamb matters to the shepherd. The shepherd knows the dangers that lurk outside of the pastures, and the naive sheep can quickly and easily get into trouble, especially when on its own. If that same lamb continues to wander off, the shepherd will break its leg so it cannot continue to wander.

This is not an act of ill will, but one of love. It is very important to notice what happens after the injury. The shepherd tends to the injury and carries the lamb everywhere it needs to go. To make things even more interesting, the bond that is created through the healing process between the lamb and shepherd is so strong that even when healed, the lamb continues to stay by the shepherd's side.

What appeared to be a harsh act was actually a loving act, which in the end benefited the lamb and deepened the lamb's trust for the shepherd. The shepherd never abandoned the sheep or let it fend for itself. No, the shepherd showed compassion and love—the shepherd didn't want to break the lamb's leg, but knew he had to in order to protect the lamb.

Like this lamb, we may wander down a path where we should not go. We may get involved in situations that are not beneficial to our well-being or spiritual growth. Sometimes God must allow drastic things to happen to catch our attention, but one thing is for certain: just like the shepherd, God will carry us through the healing process. Through our dependence upon Him, we will learn a great more about Him that we may not have known before. We will grow deeper in our knowledge of His character. We will experience a new level of His love and mercy. We will praise God even more for not letting us go down the path of destruction.

God is a nurturing God as well as a correcting God, and he balances the two perfectly.

EVERYTHING IS FOR GOD'S GLORY

God created everything for His glory, and all are to glorify Him. Our lives are not our own, but the Lord's. He made us, chose us, and has purchased us. The very fact that we are not condemned to eternity without God, but rather an eternal life and relationship with God, is enough reason for us to praise God for all eternity.

How we live life on earth displays our heart attitude and spiritual priorities. God wants us to have fun and enjoy the things of this world. God should be praised for the amazing things He created, and for the things He has given man knowledge to create, as well as for the abilities we possess, things we can do, relationships we have developed, and all the other amazing treasures and joys this world has to offer. The one thing we need to keep an eye on is that we are not to be consumed or controlled by the things of this world, because this world is not eternal.

We are to have our ultimate sights on heavenly things. This means we need to adjust our priorities, fix our attitudes, and put aside our fleshly desires. It is not bad to have wealth; however, if wealth becomes your main goal and focus, then there is a problem. It is not wrong to want to succeed and achieve; but if success is defining your worth and value, then there is a problem.

It is not wrong to be involved in various activities; but if those activities are keeping you so busy you neglect your family, God, or responsibilities, it is a problem. It is not wrong to want a title, status, or higher education; however, if you allow that title, status or educational achievement to define you and you become prideful, then you have a problem.

We could continue with things of the world we get caught up in, but I think you get the point. There is more to life than those things and at the end of the day, as Solomon says, they are all

> *"meaningless, a chasing after the wind."*
> Ecclesiastes 1-6

We do not carry our worldly status, achievements, or awards into heaven with us. Now, God can and does use people who have these things to further the kingdom while on earth. As much as I wish I had wealth and could give money to all my missionary friends or charitable organizations that I believe are advancing the kingdom of God, I have a limited amount of income and cannot give as I would like.

As much as I wish I had fame to influence more people toward the truth, I by no means have a talent that would thrust me into the limelight. As much as I may wish to travel the world, experience new cultures, and meet new people and show them the joy and freedom they can have in Christ, I am, at least for this season of my life, in one location, landlocked and living among the southern culture of North America.

So it is good that there are those who are blessed with the monies, resources, and abilities to go and serve and do the things of God to the capacity that they can. This does not mean that because I am not Billy Graham that I do not have a responsibility to evangelize to those who are in my sphere of influence. This does not mean that because I am not a missionary overseas, doing great things for the kingdom, that I am not influential in leading my family, friends, or co-workers and doing great things in my community. Absolutely not!

We are responsible for what we have been given. We are not to judge and compare or gripe and resent what God has charged one person to do over another. Paul says in Romans 9:21:

> *"Does not the potter have the right to make out of the same lump of clay some pottery for special purposes and some for common use?"*

No matter what a person's job, talents, abilities, disabilities, location, race, gender, nationality, income, or situation is, God's charge to all of us is to share the truth of salvation and to live a life that will bring God honor and glory.

> *"For we must all appear before the judgment seat of Christ, so that each of us may receive what is due us for the things done while in the body, whether good or bad."*
> 2 Corinthians 5:10

When I was younger I heard about a crown that we would receive in heaven. Being a young girl who dreamed about being a princess, this crown and royalty concept fascinated me. I dreamed of the crown I would receive and how others would see me wearing this beautiful crown of sparkling jewels. But that was my young understanding (and desire) of receiving a heavenly crown. We find several passages in scripture that discuss a crown being given to those who enter the kingdom of God:

> *"And when the Chief Shepherd appears, you will receive the crown of glory that will never fade away."*
> 1 Peter 5:4

> *"For what is our hope, our joy, or the crown in which we will glory in the presence of our Lord Jesus when he comes? Is it not you?"*
> 1 Thessalonians 2:19

> *"Now there is in store for me the crown of righteousness, which the Lord, the righteous Judge, will award to me on that day—and not only to me, but also to all who have longed for His appearing."*
>
> 2 Timothy 4:8

> *"Blessed is the one who perseveres under trial because, having stood the test, that person will receive the crown of life that the Lord has promised to those who love him."*
>
> James 1:12

> *"Do you not know that in a race all the runners run, but only one gets the prize? Run in such a way as to get the prize. Everyone who competes in the games goes into strict training. They do it to get a crown that will not last, but we do it to get a crown that will last forever. Therefore I do not run like someone running aimlessly; I do not fight like a boxer beating the air. No, I strike a blow to my body and make it my slave so that after I have preached to others, I myself will not be disqualified for the prize."*
>
> 1 Corinthians 9:24-27

So, what is this crown? The crown is made up of the heavenly things that we have accomplished in God's honor and for His glory here on earth. As you read in the scriptures above, our perseverance produces character and it is the character of God that we display in how we live that make up our crown. Just like a jewel, the works we do on this earth will be tested in the flames and undergo purification and refining.

> *"But the day of the Lord will come like a thief. The heavens will disappear with a roar; the elements will be destroyed by fire, and the earth and everything done in it will be laid bare. Since everything will be destroyed in*

> *this way, what kind of people ought you to be? You ought to live holy and godly lives as you look forward to the day of God and speed its coming. That day will bring about the destruction of the heavens by fire, and the elements will melt in the heat. But in keeping with His promise we are looking forward to a new heaven and a new earth, where righteousness dwells. So then, dear friends, since you are looking forward to this, make every effort to be found spotless, blameless and at peace with Him. Bear in mind that our Lord's patience means salvation."*
>
> 2 Peter 3:10-15

> *"By the grace God has given me, I laid a foundation as a wise builder, and someone else is building on it. But each one should build with care. For no one can lay any foundation other than the one already laid, which is Jesus Christ. If anyone builds on this foundation using gold, silver, costly stones, wood, hay or straw, their work will be shown for what it is, because the Day will bring it to light. It will be revealed with fire, and the fire will test the quality of each person's work. If what has been built survives, the builder will receive a reward. If it is burned up, the builder will suffer loss but yet will be saved—even though only as one escaping through the flames."*
>
> 1 Corinthians 3:10-15

As we have read, everything will be tested in the flames. Only the things that are holy and glorifying to God will come through the fire and be seen for what it is. Those people who are believers yet continue to live for things of this world rather than the kingdom will come through with ash. Those who served God and kept focus on heavenly things will come through with a crown.

Each crown is different and represents our life and the stewardship of the things God gave us. So, why does it matter if one comes through with a beautiful crown versus ash if both are believers and both accepted in the kingdom of God? Revelation 4:10-11 answers that question.

> *"They lay their crowns before the throne and say: "You are worthy, our Lord and God, to receive glory and honor and power, for You created all things, and by Your will they were created and have their being."*

Wow! Did you catch what that was saying? The crown-reward we receive for the God-glorifying deeds we performed while on earth, will be the very crown we present to God as an offering at His feet! I don't know about you, but I do not think my crown is worthy enough to lay before His feet. I still have a lot of growing and serving to do.

This is what I want to be sure you understand—that we are accountable for the things we do here on earth. We can use the talents, resources, and blessings God has given for His glory; to puff up our own ego or satisfy our worldly desires; or we can totally reject the giftings and give into a lie that we have nothing to offer, no purpose, or worth.

Remember, God has made some with great purpose, while some with common use—we are not to compare ourselves to others. We cannot say, "Well God, I would have done more for you if you would have given me…" No! We are accountable for what we have been given and how we use it.

> *"Again, it will be like a man going on a journey, who called his servants and entrusted his wealth to them. To one he gave five bags of gold, to another two bags, and to another one bag, each according to his ability. Then he went on his journey. The man who had received five bags of gold went at once and put his money to work and*

gained five bags more. So also, the one with two bags of gold gained two more. But the man who had received one bag went off, dug a hole in the ground and hid his master's money.

"After a long time the master of those servants returned and settled accounts with them. The man who had received five bags of gold brought the other five. 'Master,' he said, 'you entrusted me with five bags of gold. See, I have gained five more.'

"His master replied, 'Well done, good and faithful servant! You have been faithful with a few things; I will put you in charge of many things. Come and share your master's happiness!'

"The man with two bags of gold also came. 'Master,' he said, 'you entrusted me with two bags of gold; see, I have gained two more.'

"His master replied, 'Well done, good and faithful servant! You have been faithful with a few things; I will put you in charge of many things. Come and share your master's happiness!'

"Then the man who had received one bag of gold came. 'Master,' he said, 'I knew that you are a hard man, harvesting where you have not sown and gathering where you have not scattered seed. So I was afraid and went out and hid your gold in the ground. See, here is what belongs to you.'

"His master replied, 'You wicked, lazy servant! So you knew that I harvest where I have not sown and gather where I have not scattered seed? Well then, you should have put my money on deposit with the bankers, so that when I returned I would have received it back with interest.'

"'So take the bag of gold from him and give it to the one who has ten bags. For whoever has will be given more,

> *and they will have an abundance. Whoever does not have, even what they have will be taken from them. And throw that worthless servant outside, into the darkness, where there will be weeping and gnashing of teeth."*
>
> Matthew 25:14-30

The servants were entrusted with something that was not theirs. Just like the servants in this parable, we are given abilities from the Lord and they are the Lord's, not our own. If our abilities, resources, and blessings were our own, then we could do whatever we pleased. But they are not ours, for God created us and everything belongs to Him. We are stewards to the things God has given us, and we will have to account for how we lived with what was given.

It is not for us to question God regarding whom He gave what; it is for us to question ourselves in what we do with what He has given. In heaven, I won't look at what others present before God and be jealous. No, I am going to be rejoicing, because God deserves the glory of what is being presented before Him.

I also will not look at an offering one presents before God and think, "I am so glad my crown is better than that person's." No, I will be celebrating the offering being presented before our God who is deserving. When one stands before the Lord, it is strictly between that person and God regarding the offering. Only God knows what He gave for you to use on earth. All the other Saints are there to worship God with the offering that is being presented.

The heart-searching that you need to do, since you are still preparing your offering through your acts and lifestyle choices here on earth is this: are you using what has been given, and living life in a way that is glorifying God? How about glorifying God to the maximum? For those who have come to faith later in life, your past is forgiven and slate wiped clean—the question is from here on out, how are you going to live your life with what has been given to glorify God to the maximum?

Everything we do is to be for God's glory and in worship to Him, for that is why we were created. God is to be worshiped because He is God. His very existence demands it, and we also owe it because of all the things God has done for us, most importantly Him giving us eternal life with Him and not condemning us as our sins deserve. This is truly an eternal worshiping in awe, praise, and thanks that is warranted.

CONTINUE LIVING IN THE WORD

I hope this book has been a spiritually growing experience for you. This is just a start to knowing who God is, and who we are because of God. As stated throughout the book, we are because HE IS!

I encourage you to continue to read, listen, and grow in your spiritual walk with God. There is so much about Him to learn, and so much we will never fully know, because He is God and we are limited in our understanding of Him. There are many more scriptures, references, theological discussions, views, and a lot more depth to God's word.

Hebrews 4:12 says,

"For the word of God is alive and active."

God's Word, the gospel and good news of Jesus, is the only and absolute truth. It is not a religion, but a life, our life, through the redeeming work of our Savior. It is our hope and guarantee for a future—an eternal relationship with God as He originally designed. Salvation is about a relationship, not just eternal life.

God's words are powerful and reliable. There is more to scripture than what meets the eye. Scripture is relevant for any generation and across all generations. We are blessed to have scriptures in written form and should take advantage of this gift. As Deuteronomy 11:18 states, we need to put them in our heart and mind—meditate on them, memorize them, and internalize them. We need to tie or bind them to us—write notecard reminders, put post-its in visible spots, and have truth clearly before us.

I have even seen people with tattoos of a verse or image on their body as a daily reminder. There are those who wear a cross necklace or bracelet with a verse or symbol as a reminder. However you choose to be ever-present in God's words, do it! The point is to keep God's truth at the forefront, so we can maintain a right attitude, right perspective, and overcome any obstacle, test, or trial that comes our way.

Power is not in the object: the object is a reminder of the power that comes straight from God and the truth of His words.

There are so many new insights into God's word that can be revealed if we open ourselves to hear and experience it. Even across the different stages of life and season you are in, the truth of what God must reveal never ceases. What you have read in this book is by no means an end, just a beginning to the incredible things God wants to show you and teach you.

You can trust His character and rely on His faithfulness to guide you and give you what you need as you continue to live life in this world, and prepare for an eternal life in the next. In 2 Timothy 3:14-4:8, Paul writes an encouragement to Timothy, but also to all believers by saying:

> *"But as for you, continue in what you have learned and have become convinced of, because you know those from whom you learned it, and how from infancy you have known the Holy Scriptures, which are able to make you wise for salvation through faith in Christ Jesus. All Scripture is God-breathed and is useful for teaching, rebuking, correcting and training in righteousness, so that the servant of God may be thoroughly equipped for every good work.*

> *"In the presence of God and of Christ Jesus, who will judge the living and the dead, and in view of His appearing and His kingdom, I give you this charge: Preach the word; be prepared in season and out of season; correct, rebuke, and encourage—with great patience and careful instruction. For the time will come when people will not put up with sound doctrine. Instead, to suit their own desires, they will gather around them a great number of teachers to say what their itching ears want to hear. They will turn their ears away from the truth and turn aside to myths. But you, keep your head in all situations, endure hardship, do the work of an evangelist, discharge all the duties of your ministry.*
>
> *"For I am already being poured out like a drink offering, and the time for my departure is near. I have fought the good fight, I have finished the race, I have kept the faith. Now there is in store for me the crown of righteousness, which the Lord, the righteous Judge, will award to me on that day—and not only to me, but also to all who have longed for His appearing."*

This is my prayer for you; that you may take the truths you have learned and stand firm. That you may continue in your spiritual growth and run hard after God. That even when you don't feel like worshiping or obeying, that you push beyond the feeling and do what you know will glorify God.

May you surround yourself with others who are also walking with the Lord and who will lead you, be real with you, and encourage you in your faith; instead of those who will tell you what you want to hear and put human interests above God.

May you fully embrace the gifts, talents, and blessings God has given and wants to give you. May you come to love how God made you, unique in His image, and may you rest in the knowledge that it is in Him, by Him, and through Him that you can do all things.

We are because He is! Claim His truths, rest in His truths, and stand firm in His truths. What amazing plans He has in store for you and what amazing things He will do in and through you

ACKNOWLEDGMENT

Thank you for taking a moment to read this page as I share a few things from my heart and give special thanks and recognition.

When my husband put together a personal book for my step-sons on what it means to be a man, I also wanted something for my step-daughter. I had actually been desiring to write a book like this for many years, but now I had a new motivation and time limit to do so since at this time she just entered middle school and was quickly becoming a young woman.

There were many additions and redirections along the way, but as I read the finished product, I am truly thankful and blessed seeing how God was at work through the Spirit's leading. These pages have taught and challenged me in the ways I hope for her and everyone else who reads this book.

I would like to give a special thanks to my husband for challenging and inspiring me, Lisa Theriot for affirming and encouraging me, and the LifePoint women's Bible study class for letting me teach on these chapters and for your wonderful discussions and feedback.

I also want to acknowledge and give a big thanks to Katie Mullins who edited my manuscript before I submitted it for review, and to Mike Parker at WordsCraft Press for publishing my book. I am truly thankful for you all and many others whom God has used in my life to shape me as a believer and support me as I follow Him.

ABOUT THE AUTHOR

Summer McKinney holds a Masters Degree in Teaching Secondary Education, and a Masters Degree in Marriage and Family Therapy.

Summer was born and raised in Indiana, moved to Hong Kong as a short-term missionary after college, and has been back in the States for the past 14 years working with teens and adults in various ministry positions. It was during her years leading the high school girls' ministry that she decided to pursue her counseling degree.

She has a passion to equip, encourage, and challenge others as they journey in their relationship with each other, and more importantly in their relationship with the Lord.

Summer resides just outside of Nashville, Tennessee with her husband and four children, two of whom are young adults.

Also Available From

WordCrafts Press

Pro-Verb Ponderings
31 Ruminations on Positive Action
by Rodney Boyd

Morning Mist
Stories from the Water's Edge
by Barbie Loflin

Why I Failed in the Music Business
and how NOT to follow in my footsteps
by Steve Grossman

Youth Ministry is Easy!
and 9 other lies
by Aaron Shaver

Chronicles of a Believer
by Don McCain

Illuminations
by Paula K. Parker & Tracy Sugg

A Scarlet Cord of Hope
by Sheryl Griffin

www.wordcrafts.net

www.ingramcontent.com/pod-product-compliance
Lightning Source LLC
Chambersburg PA
CBHW070624300426
44113CB00010B/1653